BOOKS BY

KAY AMBROSE

THE BALLET-LOVER'S POCKET-BOOK (1945)

THE BALLET-LOVER'S COMPANION (1949)

THE BALLET-STUDENT'S PRIMER (1954)

These are BORZOI BOOKS

Published by ALFRED A. KNOPF, *in New York*

THE BALLET-LOVER'S COMPANION

THE BALLET-LOVER'S COMPANION

Æsthetics without tears for the Ballet-lover

By KAY AMBROSE

ILLUSTRATED BY THE AUTHOR

NEW YORK

ALFRED A. KNOPF

19  78

THIS IS A BORZOI BOOK,
PUBLISHED BY ALFRED A. KNOPF, INC.

PUBLISHED FEBRUARY 7, 1949
REPRINTED TEN TIMES
TWELFTH PRINTING, NOVEMBER 1978

DEDICATED TO

Celia Franca

whose inspiration and beauty are equaled
only by her love and understanding
of the art of ballet, and by her patience
with her grateful friend

KAY AMBROSE

ACKNOWLEDGMENTS

My gratitude and thanks are due to Mme Karsavina, for advice and encouragement; to Mme Volkova, for permission to watch classes and for special information concerning the training of the arms; to M. Stanislas Idzikowsky, at whose classes many of these sketches were made, and whose patience and knowledge are inexhaustible; to Mme Rambert, who carries more ballets in her head than could be contained in any book; M. Léonide Massine, for a discussion on music, and Mr. Frederick Ashton for one on choreography; Colonel de Basil and Mr. Antony Tudor for permission to watch and sketch ballets; Miss Kathleen de Vos, for practical assistance; and Mr. Walter Gore, for certain corrections.

Steps were specially demonstrated and posed by Mmes Vera Volkova, Celia Franca, Anne Lascelles, and Joyce Graeme; and by Messrs. Stanislas Idzikowsky, Poül Gnatt, Henry Danton, and Erik Brühn.

General information was extracted from countless dancers, sketches of some of whom the reader may recognize; to them all, my grateful acknowledgments.

Documentary information of all kinds, as contained in about a score of Mr. Cyril W. Beaumont's books, has been freely employed. Mr. Lionel Bradley gave invaluable assistance in providing elusive names and dates.

CONTENTS

PAGE

FOREWORD 3

i. Explanation and acknowledgment. ii. Æsthetics: the dancer's definition. iii. Æsthetics in training: cause and effect. iv. Temperament and the artist-dancer. v. The Letters *of Jean Georges Noverre. vi. On* maîtres de ballet. *vii. On the dancer as an individual. viii. General notes on teachers and pupils. ix. Preamble for the reader. x. Overture to Chapter I.*

NOTES ON THE FOLLOWING CHAPTERS . . . 17

CHAPTER

I. ON BASIC TRAINING 18

i. Deportment. ii. On physical aspects

II. ON THE USE OF THE ARMS . . . 24

i. Introduction. ii. Practical notes. iii. Long and short arms. iv. Arms and the mirror

III. ON PRACTICAL SCIENCE 30

i. Explanation. ii. Notes on balance. The use of the head in turning. iii. Notes on elevation

IV. ON PHYSICAL AND STAGE PERSPECTIVES . 36

i. Explanation. ii. Practical perspective. iii. A detail from the Mazurka in Les Sylphides. *iv. Two* tours en renversé en dehors

V. ON "LINE" 44

i. Explanation. ii. Interpretation. iii. Misinterpretation

VI. ON MUSIC AND THE DANCER . . . 50

i. Definition. ii. Demonstration (detail from Les Sylphides). *iii. The Rhythmical Dancer*

VII. ON PARTNERING 58

i. Pas-de-deux *from* Les Sylphides. *ii. Preliminary note on perspective. iii. Practical observations*

CHAPTER | | PAGE
VIII. ON CLASSIFICATION 62

i. Of ballets. ii. Of the ballerina. iii. Of the danseur. *iv. General classification*

IX. ON STYLE AND CHARACTER 68

i. On style. ii. On character. iii. Style in costume

X. PRACTICAL NOTES 74

i. On costumes and décor. *ii. On the comfort of ballet slippers. iii. On the construction and appearance of* tutus. *iv. On making up. v. On the arrangement of hair*

INDEX AND DRAMATIS PERSONÆ . . *follow page* 80

THE BALLET-LOVER'S COMPANION

PRELUDE

The vision of beauty is spontaneous, in just the same sense as the inward light of the lover. It is a state of grace that cannot be achieved by deliberate effort, though perhaps we can remove hindrances to its manifestations, for there are many witnesses that the secret of all art is to be found in self-forgetfulness. And we know that this state of grace is not to be found in the pursuit of pleasure; the hedonists have their reward, but they are in bondage to loveliness, while the artist is free in beauty.

Ananda Coomaraswamy
The Dance of Siva, chapter iv

FOREWORD

i. Explanation and acknowledgment

How many dancers deserve the title of *artist*, and how many people are entitled to say which one is an artist and which one is not?

Now, since a ballet-dancer can scarcely be a bore and an artist at the same time, one may safely admit that the public can recognize an artist, in a reasonable setting, almost on sight. There are also a number of people whose sense of values is so highly tuned that they can sense a good artist without being able to give an account of their reasons, just as some sporting people can sense a winning horse. Then there are the people of intelligence, among whom one may remark a large percentage of old ladies, who seem to know exactly who is a ballerina and who is merely masquerading under the title; and a few others.

In between the public and the groups of people of special discernment, uncertainty and prejudice are the order of the day; and in this department one finds most of the student dancers, some of the dancers themselves, and a motley collection of writers and "critics." Most of these last, having little time to spend on a conscientious study of art and its trappings, are involuntary members of the "I know what *I* like" brigade; and we are not concerned with them, nor they with us, as they are, without doubt, perfectly happy as they are.

The person to whom this book is addressed is he who is not content with adopting the prejudices of others, or with the verdict of the casual theater-goer, but who wants to discover some workable basis upon which he can form and defend his own tastes.

In order to do this, the lover of ballet secures what books he can on the subject of dancing, and before long he discovers that literature on ballet is sharply divided into certain categories. First, the books devoted to loading laurels on the popular figures of the dancing world; then the books on the technical side of dancing; then the ones on the æsthetic side. The biographies and autobiographies are almost the only ones that have perforce to combine the technical side with the æsthetic side of dancing. Perhaps the only book that intentionally combines these inseparable qualities in dancing is Noverre's *Letters on Dancing*, of which more will be said later on.

Thus it can happen that one may study dancing for years and yet remain completely in the dark with regard to what may be termed the practical ethics of dancing; and, as it has been proved a fatal mistake to study dancing and leave the ethics to take care of themselves, this book is addressed to dancers as well as to their admirers.

The prospect of addressing dancers with reference to any subject relating to dancing would have filled me with the liveliest embarrassment were it not that the dancers themselves have encouraged me to do so. They point out that the predecessor to this book, which was addressed to the followers of ballet, was much appreciated by the dancers themselves; therefore, why should not a book that is mainly concerned with dancers' problems be of interest to their audiences?

Thus emboldened, I immediately enlisted their assistance. The results are in this book. Detailed acknowledgments are, once more, out of the question; I have sought information far and wide, and a condensed version of my findings appears in these pages. Sometimes I am indebted to several people for one sketch, and to a dozen more for the notes underneath it. Generally speaking, I have made acknowledgments to the people whose time I have stolen to the greatest extent.

I cannot find words with which to express my gratitude to all those who have so unselfishly given me their help. Their enthusiasm, their demonstrations, their suggestions of every kind; their forbearance when I asked involved questions demanding simple answers; their impartiality in sending me from one to another for information; their modesty, which, allied to their love of their art, makes of them a group of people worthy of that respect and love which it is my privilege, and that of countless others, to accord them.

ii. Æsthetics: the dancer's definition

The word *æsthetics*, according to the dictionary, means "the feeling of beauty in objects, the principles of taste and art." If there was an alternative, a less-abused word that was equally suitable, I should gladly use that instead. *Æstheticism* is a word that is most used by those who understand it least; consequently, at present it has what may be termed horn-rimmed associations, and also a vague connection with pompousness and *chi-chi.*

Nevertheless, it is this strong feeling for beauty that first causes a child to want to become a ballet-dancer (a desire for physical movement alone usually indicates a career in sport). If genuine, and properly nurtured, that feeling for art will survive and become the æsthetic quality of the finished dancer. As the years go by, however, and the technique of ballet-dancing becomes increasingly difficult to acquire, that priceless feeling for beauty has to survive a great deal of hard, mechanical training; one might almost say drudgery; and sometimes, although the dancer survives, the feeling does not. The involuntary reaction to music, the joy of movement, instead of being developed in the course of the training, become submerged in a torrent of militant physical technicalities.

Then we get a dancer who is "cold." If he knows there is something wrong with his work, he will suffer agonies; if he is perfectly satisfied with himself, then he remains an uninteresting performer and an irritating personality.

Therefore it is of the greatest importance to attend to the æsthetic side of a dancer's training. It is quite useless to adopt the unproductive attitude that "either you've *got* the feeling or you just *haven't*." If that feeling has once been yours, then there is no reason why it should not be encouraged and developed, instead of curbed and extinguished.

Æsthetics, for the ballet-dancer, can and should be included in the course of ordinary training. Their study consists in the perpetual consideration of the practical education of the artist-dancer, and the perpetual adjustment of this education, by the preceptor, to suit each separate pupil.

The æsthetic quality in dancing is the one that distinguishes the artist from the technical acrobat. The difference is that which exists between boredom and stimulation; in the theater that is the difference between life and death.

iii. Æsthetics in training: cause and effect

The existence of the æsthetic quality in dancing having been established, the next step is to confirm its identity. One way of doing this is to attempt to analyze the precise qualities of certain great artist-dancers; but this would get us little further, as it is individuality that distinguishes the artist; and although the most minute consideration of each of the great dancers is an inspiration to us, it is doubtful whether, in this way, we should be able to draw any workable conclusion as to the very essence of this most transient form of art. As it is with this essential artistry that this book is concerned, we will consider the matter, not from the aspect of the great dancers, but from its very source; that is to say, from the point at which a student who is possessed of all the natural attributes of the great dancer embarks on his serious training as an artist.

His training as an artist should take place concurrently with his technical training; indeed, the two considerations should be synonymous. And here we come to the root of the matter; it is obvious that when these two factors, art and technique, become separated from each other, ballet ceases to be an art.

The essence of all art is to sound a chord that will find an echo of sympathy in the majority of its spectators or auditors. In ballet the deep satisfaction we feel after a successful *pas-de-deux* is due to certain ideals that come to life in all of us; perhaps we may say "all the world loves lovers," and thus see it proved. Conversely, after a mechanically performed *pas-de-deux* we feel vaguely embarrassed and slightly guilty, as if we had been watching two inexperienced lovers through a keyhole. Anger, jealousy, love, avarice, in their realistic form, are not the concern of the artist-dancer. The passions must be interpreted poignantly, rather than robustly, so that in watching the dancers we feel for them, because they are feeling for us, and expressing that feeling through their movements.

The dancer who can touch us in this manner is one who has mastered subtleties and inflections of movement, which, while they could never be taught to an insensitive pupil, can be fostered and developed in the normal student during the course of his or her ballet training.

The bulk of the practical material that this book contains deals with the way in which subtleties in training can have a direct bearing on the ultimate subtleties of the dancer's performance.

At first sight, the sketches, diagrams, and explanations may seem to have little to do with the development of art; nevertheless, each section contains an example of misinterpretation. In nearly every one of these cases the misinterpretation consists of failure to perceive the real purpose of the object in question; for example, performing a beautiful pose and showing the wrong view of it to the audience.

This travesty is the result of allowing the æsthetic object of dancing to become separated from the purely mechanical object.

I have had to try to separate certain indivisible elements in ballet in order to consider the construction of the whole; but it is as well to remember that, in practice, it is as difficult as it is inadvisable to separate the æsthetic from the purely mechanical components of dancing.

To dance without feeling is not to dance at all; that is to say, artistically it is not ballet, however many *pirouettes*, *entrechats*, etc., the dancer may perform. Conversely, one who possesses quantities of emotion and who cannot master the training of a great academic technique should shun a career in ballet, and only attempt "Greek" dancing, or the various "expressionistic" forms of the dance, where the delight of the performer himself is the first consideration. For untrammeled emotion is like an untrained body—unwieldy and unsuitable for the ballet stage.

During the centuries which have seen the development of ballet, preponderance has been given alternately to technical and æsthetic considerations. At the present time the æsthetic quality in dancing is receiving too much of the wrong sort of attention, with writers and spectators so engrossed with their own reactions that the realities of a ballet performance are apt to escape them.

The very basis of education is emotional reserve. That is why so many teachers and directors confuse real feeling with the vulgarity of exhibitionism; and many more, while possessing sincere and deep feeling themselves, shrink from analyzing their own hearts, in order to help their pupils to develop along the same lines.

iv. Temperament and the artist-dancer

For all general purposes, the term *artist*, used in conjunction with a dancer, has become a purely complimentary one, even as the word *artiste*, as it is used today, simply implies that someone is pursuing a theatrical career. The term *temperament* is widely used to describe the nervous and irritable characteristics attributed to all those associated with the stage.

The object of this book being to prove that, although the terms *dancer* and *artist* should be synonymous, this is not always the case, a study of the qualities of the genuine artist has been attempted; and this cannot be completed without reference to temperament.

As we have seen, if a dancer is not an artist as well as a trained performer of leaps, postures, and steps, then there is little to choose between him and an acrobat (indeed, if the latter is passionately attached to his work, he may well prove the better artist of the two).

The quality that makes an artist of a dancer is one that defies summarization. It is closely allied to the passions, and consists of a mixture of sensitivity of the mind, acuteness of the senses, and physical control of the body and features.

In the first place, if you possess the soul of an artist, it is useless in dancing unless you are able to express it in a convincing and clearly visible form to an audience.

Secondly, if you have remarkable physical and muscular gifts, superb control and elevation, an audience will remain ignorant of your real powers if you have an apparently cold or placid disposition and are at a loss how to convey any emotion in the form of movement; that is to say, if you lack the right temperament.

In both these cases the dancer would earn the title of artist if he balanced his natural gifts by studying those qualities which are not naturally his. The third contingent, however, are incapable of any feeling other than that of physical discomfort; consequently, with no knowledge of the inner meaning of the word, they set about copying its external characteristics, and that is one of the most unpleasant phenomena that can be seen. They confuse weakness with strength, comedy with romance, and tantrums with tragedy; in short, they mistake temper for temperament.

It is useless to point out that they should renounce the pursuit of art. They cannot understand the term, and, by the same token, neither can they appreciate their own shortcomings. They can, however, talk business, and this is the explanation behind so many mediocre ballet companies today, and so many saddened and restless artist-dancers.

Genuine temperament, then, is a form of acute mental sensitivity peculiar to the genuine artist. As such people are, more often than not, persons of good taste, they usually have too much consideration to inflict on other people those wild scenes which are popularly, and wrongly, understood to be the main outward signs of genius. Nevertheless, they feel so strongly about certain matters that sometimes their sense of artistic outrage amounts to violent physical pain, and under these circumstances the smallest incident may be the only apparent cause of a storm. This occasional tempest at first frightens the insensitive spectator, then impresses him. He resolves to give an imitation himself when opportunity offers; and this is mainly how the word *temperament* has become so grossly misunderstood and misused.

It is a bold writer who will dare to place on record that true temperamental qualities cannot be cultivated. But it can be stated categorically that nothing is to be gained by imitating the outward signs of temperament in others. To take an instance: a painter who lives in squalor is not to be congratulated on the condition of his studio, but on his work; those who think to improve their own work by imitating the squalor are obviously unintelligent, and do much to degrade their art into what should be their own personal disrepute.

The best breeding-ground in which true temperamental qualities can be cultivated is in the liberal use of the brain. Study music, study literature and the arts; in moderation, study yourself; bring intelligence to bear on all you do. Thus you will develop your own standards, without which you will be incapable of judging yourself, or anyone else. Instead of harboring that negative sensation, jealousy, you will learn to profit by the example of great dancers; and even if you don't become a great dancer in your own estimation, yet if you work thus hard and sincerely, you will find that other people's opinion of your progress will grow in proportion to your own self-respect.

v. *The Letters of Jean Georges Noverre*

It would be idle to attempt to write any survey of the practical æsthetics of ballet without continual recourse to the *Letters on Dancing and Ballets* (*Lettres sur la danse*) of Jean Georges Noverre (1727–1810). This great man has been called "the Shakespeare of the dance" by Garrick, and likened to Prometheus by Voltaire, who affirms that Noverre should "first make men, and then make them move."

I have heard disillusioned artists and dancers say that "it is so depressing to read that Noverre's problems in the eighteenth century were just the same as ours today." This attitude is one which shows that the real value of the *Letters* has not been perceived, and it is to be hoped that the majority of readers will take advantage of the comforting reflection that not only had Noverre found the cause of and the practical solution to those very problems, but he left us an account of how he was able to effect his revolution, "which," he says, in one of his prefaces to his published *Letters*, "is as great as the musical revolution effected by Gluck."

Noverre was one of those rare people whose character effectually combines common sense with good taste and a flaming and passionate love of his art, which he was sufficiently level-headed to control. On the stage he presented the superb results of this well-balanced mixture of taste, learning, and originality to the public of his day; the present-day reader can study his analyses of his own works in this remarkable book.

There are few people who can read Shakespeare without finding in his work continual observations and allusions that bear directly upon present-day events and circumstances. In the same way, the lover of ballet and art will find that his is indeed a strange problem if Noverre has not dealt with it and suggested its cause and solution. The *Letters* encompass the dancer, his physique, his training, and even his diet; the construction of ballets from every point of view; quarrels, jealousies, and conceits. Noverre pursues his creed, for the most part, with measured calm, but flashes of wit and temper occasionally combine to make one admire the man for his courage. He made terrible enemies, but his unselfish love for his art overrode social considerations at a gallop, even when he knew he was risking his own financial position and immediate career.

These *Letters* have been ably and subtly translated, printed, and published by Cyril W. Beaumont, to whom both dancers and their admirers are already so deeply indebted for his own conscientious and informative books. Noverre should be the delight of the ballet-lover, and of any connoisseur; a constant inspiration to the dancer; and a veritable bible to the choreographer. He is much quoted in this book.

vi. On maîtres-de-ballet

The popular practice of pigeonholing sections of society, which stipulates that all genuine professors are vague, all real artists dirty, and so forth, would have us believe that all bona-fide teachers of dancing should possess and display a vicious temper. Instances of malevolence are cited, not with the purpose of shocking the hearer, but rather to impress him with the great gifts of the teacher.

Thus it becomes necessary to insist that the behavior of a teacher is only incidental to the quality of his teaching. (The often-repeated story of the famous conductor who seized the first fiddle's violin and broke it to show his disapproval of the orchestra's performance has done little to improve that conductor's musical reputation, which was presumably built up on his performance as a conductor, and not on personal attacks on his musicians, as the sensation-mongers would like us to believe.)

Because one teacher is vociferous and condemnatory and has good pupils, it does not follow that one who is gentle and courteous does not also obtain excellent results. A young pupil may learn more easily from one than from the other, but this is due to the obvious difference between the nervous and the lazy pupil.

The mature pupil should be able to learn something from every established teacher.

But I have known a woman, whose daughter had learned hitherto from a somewhat loquacious teacher, to take her away from the class of a celebrated Continental *maître-de-ballet.* "He never made any corrections, and hardly spoke at all," she complained.—If dancers were made by speaking, what a wealth of virtuosos there would be!

N.B. In English, the term *maître-de-ballet* means a teacher of dancing. Used in a French context, it also means a choreographer.

vii. On the dancer as an individual

It has been very difficult to divide this book into separate sections. Each problem seemed to spring from the same cause and, when logically unraveled, to have basically the same solution.

For example: let us compare the dancer who is gifted technically and physically, but who remains unnoticed on the stage, an unsatisfactory performer; and the dancer who gives a marvelous performance, but who has an unreliable technique and certain physical disadvantages. At first sight, one might suppose that their problems have quite different causes; on consideration, one realizes that they have probably received exactly the same sort of training, which suited neither, and that their teachers were too inflexible to develop their separate talents and help them, at the same time, to remedy their inherent disadvantages. Therefore, these two dancers, so widely different, are suffering from precisely the same malady. It is only superficially that they should be treated differently from each other; basically, that very difference should spring from one source, which is the diagnosis and development of the individual.

Clearly, if I were to pursue this line of reasoning, this book would run into several volumes, while the point itself would become obscured. Therefore, in this case and throughout these pages, I have confined myself to the introduction of carefully chosen lines of thought that I sincerely believe will be profitable to the reader if he develops them himself.

viii. General notes on teachers and pupils

J. G. Noverre accused the dancers of his day of indolence and sloth. One of the reasons he named to prove their laziness was their refusal to pay any attention to a certain treatise on dancing by a M. de Cahusac. This treatise dealt with dancing in its æsthetic sense as well as in general; and (as the reader will have discovered) since even the simplest discussion of æsthetics in dancing means much earnest thought, the dancers were not disposed to take the trouble to study this volume. They poured scorn on de Cahusac and poked fun at him and his beliefs; and Noverre, confronted by dancers who had learned dancing "less to escape a more tranquil profession than to enjoy the pleasures they think to encounter . . ." and finding it difficult to carry out his choreographic intentions with such material, set about making their ears tingle with conspicuous success.

Today in the world of dancing the same sort of situation exists. It has become a habit among dancers to complain of bad teachers, and vice versa; but most of the persons concerned have shown themselves to be more than reluctant to practice any exacting method of dancing that requires the students to attempt difficult but unsensational feats, rather than to display those movements which they can already master. Even as in Noverre's day, they readily attend classes that afford them an opportunity to show their natural elegance and talents; but they do not seem prepared to try to master what cannot be easily performed, in the way of *adages* and exercises.

Anyone who speaks with favor of the system of the late Maestro Enrico Cecchetti will find himself in the predicament of some hard-working student or scholar who is considered a traitor by his lazier fellows because he works hard and conscientiously and causes the professor to make critical comparisons.

To get the best out of Cecchetti, this master must be thoroughly understood. Any scientific experiment is apt to go astray if the equipment is mishandled by the experimenter. Cecchetti's system of exercises and *enchaînements* is not designed for elegance in the classroom, but for the acquisition of strength and that complete control without which a dancer's stage performance will always be, at best, erratic.

It is clear that a dancer should always do his best on the stage, but it is a mistake to think that he should only make supreme physical efforts when before the public. The classroom is the place in which physical effort, for its own sake, should be practiced. On the stage the dancer should use his utmost skill and artistry, but he should only exert those technical powers which are already his; he should never attempt any physical experiments in public, when he is uncertain of the result.

Therefore, the dancer who has a great technical control has a great advantage over the dancer who has brilliant technical capabilities, but who lacks control; indeed, on the ballet stage the virtuoso often seems to be surpassed in technique by the purely skillful dancer. Furthermore, when a dancer who has traded on his technical gifts and has not troubled himself with the science of dancing in its musical and artistic aspects reaches maturity, he immediately starts to lose all his powers, as he has absolutely nothing with which to replace the ardor and unconscious physical *attaque* of youth. Whereas the "scientific" dancer, who has learned to weave spells as well as to perform physical wonders, who does everything consciously, can grow greater and greater, as Léonide Massine has shown us.

Properly interpreted, the Cecchetti method teaches just that control. With such an ally as technical and physical mastery on his side, the dancer has far greater freedom to experiment with the expressive and artistic side of theatrical art and gains the greatest profit from the lessons and examples of other great teachers and dancers.

There are many great teachers of dancing now living, and it would be ridiculous, and contrary to my intention, to try to stipulate that they should all teach in the Cecchetti style. Individuality in teachers is as important as individuality in dancers; the fame of both dancer and teacher should live on through the work of his pupils. Cecchetti's pupils included the divine Karsavina; and he was the *maître-de-ballet* of the glittering array of prodigious artists which took Paris and the world by storm during the reign of the artistic mammoth Diaghilev. When Cecchetti died, however, his work did not die with him, for he had established certain rules, methods, and routines for every day of the week, which have survived his death; since when he has, as it were posthumously, trained many pupils with outstanding success.

That the method of Enrico Cecchetti was not entrusted entirely to the erratic memory of man is due to the conscientious work of the celebrated dancer and teacher Stanislas Idzikowski and Cyril Beaumont, who placed the dancing world even deeper in their debt by compiling books during the lifetime of Cecchetti in which his method is excellently propounded.

It would be entirely false if I were to give the impression that dancers should only pay attention to teachers of the Cecchetti method. It cannot be made too clear that a bad *maître-de-ballet* can harm his pupils through any system he cares to affect, whereas a good teacher can elevate his pupils through his own example, personality, and system. When Jules Perrot presented Carlotta Grisi to a delighted public in the 1830's as his pupil and partner, there is no doubt that the system he employed to train this legendary dancer was none other than his own.

In conclusion, there seems to be an unspoken belief among ballet pupils that it is their teachers who must do all the hard work. That is to say, it is assumed that if the pupil attends regular classes of a given number of hours a day, he will therefore improve; if he does not, it is the teacher's fault.

But it must be stressed that even if a dancer works daily until he is sweating profusely and tired out, if he is habitually lazy with his mind he will not improve, and the teacher cannot be blamed.

ix. Preamble for the reader

To make unqualified statements is a risky business, as it paves the way for contradiction and offense. But if I give a full explanation of every point I wish to make, in order to prevent possible misunderstanding, this book will assume enormous proportions. Therefore, as I cannot always give even two sides of a many-sided question, I have arranged the following chapters so that they substantiate and elucidate one another.

It is the exception that often proves the rule, and this must be admitted; but it should remain an admission and not become a policy. Any technique evolved from exceptions alone would be a most unreliable affair. Whereas the performance of a certain dancer may justify any peculiarities of his training, in this book we are concerned only with those rules which can be applied generally and with safety.

Where the demonstrations of particular dances and steps are concerned, these are included as an illustrative example of the point in question and are not submitted as a model that must be copied in every detail. The intelligent reader will easily appreciate that the purpose of such examples is more analytical than dictatorial.

In the course of these analyses the attempt has been made to present the material so that it will be of interest to the dancer and at the same time will not be too technical to amuse and interest the casual reader and those lovers of dancing who want to develop their own standards but who "simply don't know where to begin."

x. Overture to Chapter I

The technical steps displayed in *The Ballet-Lover's Pocket-Book* are danced by figures that, although some of them are immature, are all well proportioned. Unfortunately, in real life few people are perfectly made, and dancers are no exception to this rule.

In some cases the fault lies with nature and can be cured by a careful and clever teacher; in others the faults are due to bad training itself, which amounts to a number of bad habits, the effects of which are notoriously hard to eradicate.

Bowlegs and knock-knees can, in many cases, be cured, but when the malformation takes the form of curved thigh-bones, for example, this can only be cured in earliest infancy, if then.

The reader may want to know what is the link between such dry, physical facts and the study of the æsthetic side of dancing: a link there is, and a most significant one. Any dancer who has had to combat an obstinate physical disadvantage gains much strength of character, which another, a perfectly formed and gifted dancer, may easily lack. But the dancer with natural facility—unless nature has also gifted her with unusual modesty, sense, and determination—may present that not unusual phenomenon: the raving beauty who is artistically dumb.

Therefore, those dancers who are dispirited by some physical disadvantage should take heart. If ill health could prevent a dancer from dancing, the theatrical world would have lost Anna Pavlova; if the struggle with technique could not be won by courage, perseverance, and artistry, Olga Preobrajenskaya's brilliance would never have been seen, and the ballet would have been impoverished of her marvelously trained pupils, of whom familiar examples are Baronova, Riabouchinska, and Toumanova.

It is true that many artists of all kinds are basically lazy, and that, lacking some incentive, they may not reveal their real powers. It is equally true that artists who have suffered privation have a wider field of inspiration and a better conception of human values than their luckier fellows.

It is also true that privation has, in the past, prevented innumerable artists from doing creative work, and thus deprived us of much of that which we can ill afford to lose.

All great artists provide material for their successors to study. It is those who have made deductions and discoveries, and thus established certain rules, who have left us clear lessons that may be learned today; it is those whose genius flamed, unexplained and unquenchable, who provide us with the inspiration and the temerity to attempt the impossible.

NOTES ON THE FOLLOWING CHAPTERS

1. Technical terms

Throughout the following chapters I have done my best to avoid any save the simplest technical terms, and most of these are clearly illustrated. There is no space here to include an illustrated glossary of steps; but the reader can be referred to *The Ballet-Lover's Pocket-Book*, which, uniform with this volume, contains illustrations and descriptions of all steps used, but not described, in these pages.

2. "Les Sylphides"

Presented in 1909, and still in the repertoire of any leading company, extracts from this ballet have been chosen to prove many points in this book: (a) because most ballet-lovers have seen it and are likely to do so again, and (b) because Fokine's sensitive choreography, constructed with the simplicity of the great master, has suffered much clumsy handling in recent years. It is to be hoped that the ballet-lover will pause in future before he accuses of dullness what should be a moving and beautiful work.

3. The "awkward" dancers

In some cases it may seem that the worst aspect of a dancer has been chosen in preference to the best. Such examples are not chosen from any uncharitable motive, but to establish a certain point with force and clarity.

4. The angles of the figures

To avoid unnecessary foreshortening of the limbs, I have drawn the figure standing at an angle of 45° to the spectator whenever this does not interfere with the continuity of a step. (E.g., *à la 4*e, p. 36.)

5. To "read" the technical sketches

Turn this book upside down and place it on the ground in front of you. Then the right and left sides of the sketched figure will correspond with your own.

CHAPTER I. ON BASIC TRAINING

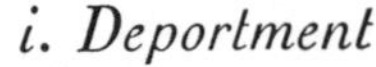

i. Deportment

The girl on the left has had a bad training. She has always done her best, when at the *barre*, to comply with her instructions, and these have been something like this: "Pull your shoulders back, look up, give yourself a long neck, make yourself as tall as you can, try to make your shoulder-blades meet, tuck your tail in and turn your feet out."

Some results of this basic training are as follows: an apparently short neck; a flat chest, from undue stretching of the pectoral muscles; weak ribs, and consequently bad breathing; a protuberant diaphragm, which accentuates an arched or "dancer's" back; this, in turn, draws attention to an overdeveloped and tilted posterior. The thighs and legs tend to thicken and are, in fact, crooked. The dismal list is concluded by weak and rolling feet, because the dancer is trying to turn them out independently; and this is not possible when the hips and knees are turned in. She is strained in appearance, and is leaning heavily on the *barre*. Her career will be short, as she will soon be "muscle-bound." Her movements are hampered and restricted by the unnecessary bulkiness occasioned by her training, and she easily becomes exhausted.

The girl on the right looks far more at ease. She is neither rigid nor slack, because her shoulders are neither round nor overdrilled. The stomach and posterior are both drawn in, and when the lower pelvis is also advanced, it is unnecessary to consider "tucking the tail in" as a separate objective. Her head is level on her neck and shoulders, and this is the result of trying "to push out the back of her neck" rather than curving it by raising her chin. She is firmly placed, because she has not concentrated solely on turning out her feet, but also her hips and knees; the feet then turn out by themselves, and it is only necessary to make sure that the ankles do not roll, and that the feet grip the floor almost as f the toes were fingers and perfectly flat on the ground. Her hand is lightly placed on the *barre*. It will be noticed that her weight is evenly distributed between her two feet, whereas the center of gravity of the girl on the left is well forward, most of her weight being taken on her front foot and on her hand on the *barre*. Although the girl on the right ooks more restful than her companion, he works just as hard. She knows that ne of the arts of ballet is to conceal all ffort.

In dancing, overdeveloped muscles re more a sign of weakness than of trength. The girl on this page has control of all her movements, and has therefore an unsuspected store of endurance.

ii. On physical aspects

Nearly every dancer conforms to one of two distinct physical categories: (i) the *close-legged* dancer (featuring the *jarreté* formation of the legs), or (ii) the *bow-legged* dancer (the *arqué* formation). Although both these groups may be described as physically defective, it will be seen that the most important matter is to decide to which group a certain dancer belongs; and to make sure that his training does not accentuate his particular defect, but lessens it, and helps him to overcome all the physical obstacles which would prevent him from enjoying that precision, freedom of movement, and *abandon* * which are ever the delight of the successful dancer and of his audience.

Clearly, it is not only inadvisable but distinctly dangerous to give exactly the same exercises to dancers who have totally dissimilar physiques. Noverre says: "*Is it not essential to lead them* [the dancers] *to the same end but by different roads?*" This maxim does not apply solely to bow-legged or close-legged dancers, but to the multiple irregularities of physique, bad habits, and involuntary failings with which nature afflicts every human being, and against which dancers and their teachers must wage an unceasing battle. The dancer and his teacher must decide between them upon special exercises and deportment to meet each case. The two examples of leg-formation dealt with in this chapter show the barest essentials of an extremely complicated subject.

The *close-legged dancer*, as the name implies, is one whose thighs and knees are pressed closely together, while the ankles are a considerable distance apart. The hips are usually narrow, and the insteps high and beautiful, but often weak. The girls stand on their *pointes* very easily, but need very strongly blocked shoes with very stiff soles.

This type of dancer is usually extremely loose-limbed and supple; and it is painful to see him continually doing exercises that will make him still more supple, which in this case means still weaker. He seizes every excuse to perform quantities of *grands battements*, the "splits," etc. He can throw his legs very high, and this appearance of height is increased by the fact that his knees bend, as it were, the wrong way. Instead of working to strengthen and control his movements, he allows the ill-considered envy of his companions to induce him to exploit his looseness, until his legs look like sticks of damp macaroni, and he becomes unable to regulate his movements to conform to the demands of musical tempi.

---

* an appearance of careless spontaneity.

Instead of this condition of repose and self-satisfaction, the close-legged dancer should study unceasingly the best methods of making his legs appear as straight as possible. To this end he must turn out his thighs and perform great numbers of *ronds de jambe*, strongly and with vigor, which will help to straighten and strengthen his knees; in addition he must practice *échappés á la seconde*, and, using the mirror to judge himself, he must relax his knee-joints sufficiently so that his legs appear straight when in reality they are not so. When he practices *entrechats*, beats, etc., he may again relax his knees slightly, and thus avoid the unpleasant spectacle presented by the thighs and knees when they seem to roll one upon the other.

If he works hard and unceasingly upon these lines, it will be hard to tell that he suffers from any physical defect; in fact, this training may even effect a genuine cure; and he will delight the spectator with that grace and flowing nobility of movement which is his heritage.

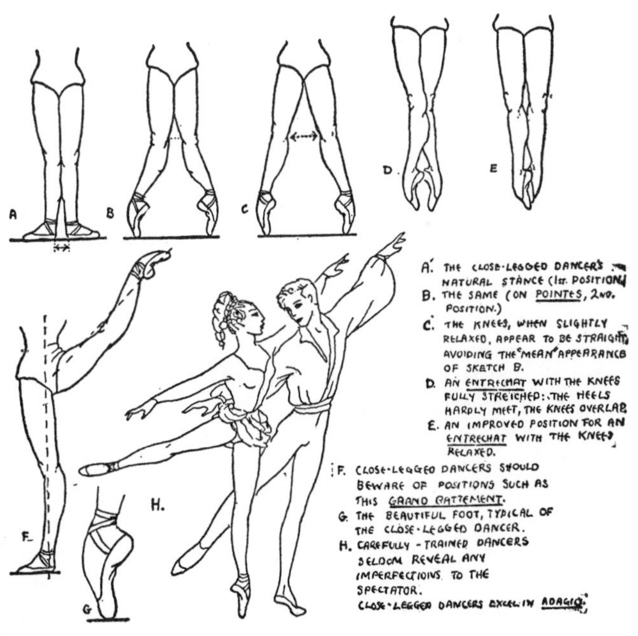

Those who belong to the *bow-legged* group of dancers are seldom tempted to take life easily. At the outset of their careers they are usually envious of the close-legged dancers' suppleness and easy grace of their elegant feet, and general appearance; this is bad for both groups, as it encourages the close-legged dancer to believe in his own perfections, and causes the bow-legged one to bemoan those physical characteristics which can so easily become advantages if intelligently trained and used.

The bow-legged dancer is usually strongly built, often wide across the hips, vigorous, and in all ways opposite to the other group. His chief occupation should be to try to bring together those parts of his legs which are too greatly separated, principally his knees. To bring this about, he also must turn out his thighs as much as possible. He is usually "stiff," by reason of his natural strength, and constantly must practice *grands battements* and all exercises that will loosen his joints. He must stretch his knees as much as possible on all occasions when the legs should be straight. This task, of making his legs appear quite straight, is further complicated by long, flat feet, which occasion much sorrow and despair to the owner—especially in the case of a girl, who may have difficulty in rising and remaining on her *pointes.* (If such a girl is reading these pages, she should turn to the chapter headed "Practical Notes," where she will find much to help her with this problem.)

The advantages of the bow-legged dancer are many and heartening. Those long, flat, strong feet enable him to jump great heights and to land as lightly as a feather. (As one *maître-de-ballet* philosophically pointed out, "If you can jump, then you usually have a big behind, but there is no need to let it stick out!") His *entrechats* and beats are brilliant, because the "light" between his legs accentuates the movements of the feet when *en l'air;* which effect the close-legged dancer has to try to cultivate, by relaxing his knees.

He has that elastic resilience in steps of elevation which is called *ballon,* and which is one of the most sought-after qualities in dancing. The combination of this soft quality in leaping and the sharp brilliance of his beats makes him an inspiring performer in *temps d'allégro.* To offset this facility, he should practice the slow and precise movements in *adagio* with particular care.

The great dancer Nijinsky possessed such astonishing powers of elevation that his leaps have now become a legend. That he also had remarkably developed thighs, and the most unusual feet, is an accesory fact; but those physical peculiarities might have modified his fame as a performer, were it not that his artistry and religious application to his work rendered his physical peculiarities unnoticeable on the stage, though remarkable in the photographs of him that we study today.

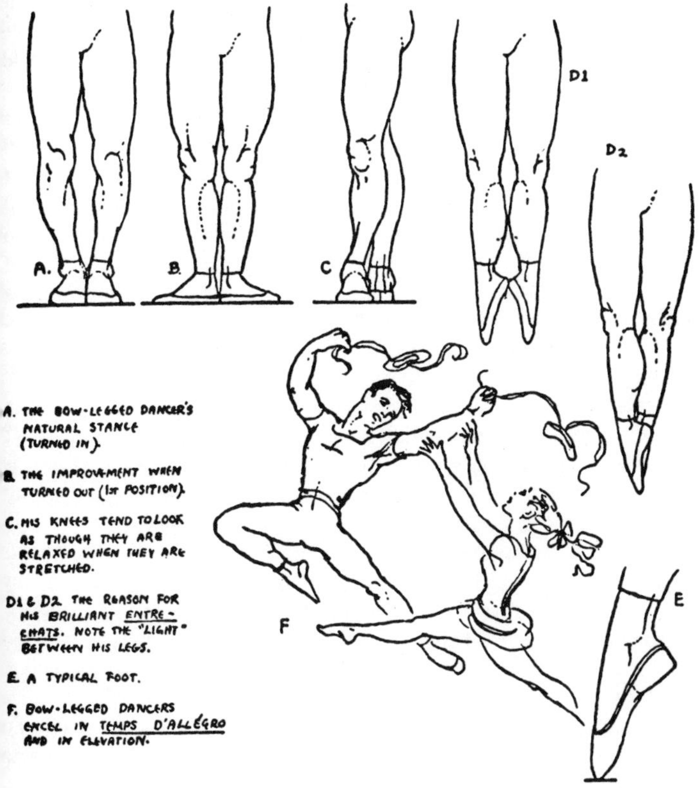
A.
B.
C
D1
D2
E
F
A. THE BOW-LEGGED DANCER'S NATURAL STANCE (TURNED IN).
B. THE IMPROVEMENT WHEN TURNED OUT (1ST POSITION).
C. HIS KNEES TEND TO LOOK AS THOUGH THEY ARE RELAXED WHEN THEY ARE STRETCHED.
D1 & D2 THE REASON FOR HIS BRILLIANT ENTRE-CHATS. NOTE THE "LIGHT" BETWEEN HIS LEGS.
E A TYPICAL FOOT.
F. BOW-LEGGED DANCERS EXCEL IN TEMPS D'ALLÉGRO AND IN ELEVATION.

CHAPTER II. ON THE USE OF THE ARMS

i. Introduction

In the days when the *danseuse's* skirts touched the ground, it was generally assumed that ladies possessed but one leg apiece, and whether that leg was straight or otherwise was of little account. In consequence, their arms came in for the greatest part of their attention; in fact, in his *Letters* Noverre cites "voluptuous arms" as one of the "inevitable rocks upon which criticism founders." Today it is to be doubted whether the average standard of our dancer's arm-movements would dazzle the critic sufficiently to blind him to any other shortcomings.

As a rule, a dancer's legs take up by far the largest proportion of his attention; exercises for the arms are performed simply on the assumption that the result will benefit the arms, *quod erat demonstrandum.* It follows, therefore, that dancers' arm-movements are more haphazard than otherwise—a state of affairs much deplored by Carlo Blasis, who affirmed in 1830 that the dancer who neglected to study his arms had failed to realize that the arms form a frame that sets off the movements of the body and legs; and that ill-considered arms mar the dancer's performance, in the same way that the value of a picture that is unsuitably framed, or not framed at all, is "unquestionably destroyed."

Directly the fair sex have been allowed to display their legs, their arm-movements have suffered. This is proved by the present-day performances of period plays and films, in which the leading ladies look so ill at ease, while the more mature actresses, playing the roles of older women, look perfectly at home. You cannot wear, for example, an Edwardian dress and expect to look like an Edwardian lady if you cannot make pleasing lines with your shoulders and arms.

Perhaps in the days of Taglioni and Gardel dancers were taught to use their arms as part of their social education and could thus afford to concentrate on their feet and legs without the ungainly results to be seen today.

Our contemporary lack of beautiful and compelling arms is partly due to the dancer's preoccupation with his legs, and partly to his tendency to confine his energies to the exploitation of his natural gifts. If he can jump, if he has a "marvelous *arabesque*," he continues to try to make himself conspicuous by these means alone, never pausing to consider that the dancer who is also an artist will even relinquish a part of his special gifts in order to improve his general standard.

ii. Practical notes

The possessors of abnormally long or abnormally short arms should bear in mind that the less time they spend with their arms fully extended, the better. This is not to say that they must avoid all postures that include the extended positions of the arms, for without them dancing could not take place. It means, quite simply, that dancers who have arms that are out of proportion to their bodies should make those movements which precede and follow the extension of their arms as graceful and studied as possible.

To illustrate this point: note that the performer of an *arabesque* should reserve his supreme effort for the moment that occurs just before he relaxes his pose, in which he stretches the line from toe to fingertip so that it is as long and graceful as can be. If he were to adopt this excessively stretched position with undue haste, its principal value would be lost, for the spectator will not have had time to watch the position "grow." *The beauty and harmony of movement itself will legitimately distract an audience from the study of physical proportions.* Thus the spectator can be encouraged to say "that dancer moves beautifully," rather than "that dancer standing stock still has short arms."

The possessors of normally proportioned arms can make them appear both lovely and eloquent if they hold them with the wrists and forearms softly aligned, the hands suitably and simply controlled, and the elbows rounded and supported. Those with short arms should take care to hold their hands to give the greatest possible appearance of length, but must be watchful lest the hands become stiff and ungraceful in movement. Those with long arms should curve their wrists and elbows, while remaining on their guard against unbecoming angles; they must control their hands, which, as they are usually long and elegant, are inclined to "flap" and to appear disagreeably affected.

All dancers desirous of improving their arms must regard the mirror with the utmost caution. For instance, a dancer may be convinced that he or she has solved the problem of long arms by undue bending of the elbows and wrists. As the height of the shoulders and arms is near the eye-level, the mirror will make this experiment appear successful. But the view from an altered eye-level—from the stalls or circle—may well be disastrous for the dancer. (See p. 28.)

In conclusion, any dancer who makes a serious study of the arms will be amply rewarded by a far more authoritative bearing and an immense improvement in the apparent height of elevation, and so on; but he or she must be prepared to take infinite pains.

iii. Long and short arms

The girls in the sketches below may have had short arms or long arms—who can tell? What does it matter? If there were any shortcomings, they remain a secret from us, as from the lithographers. To dispel the idea that any untrained arms can look like those of Mlles Grahn and Grisi, the reader is invited to try to imitate these two positions.

On the right: "Imagine you are trying to hug an enormous hoop." Figs. 1, 2, and 3 show a bird's-eye view of this experiment. 1 and 2 are incorrect; 3 is successful; 3A, the correct angle for the hoop, seen in elevation.

4. A normal arm, extended, but *not* in a ballet position.
5. A "double-jointed" arm, extended as above.
6. A misinterpretation of a supported elbow, which would lead to hard, muscular arms and movements.

7 & 8. Whatever the position of the hands, the elbows should remain rounded and supported, whether the hand is palm downwards (7), or as in the 2nd position of the arms (8). Compare the sketch of Camargo on p. 51 with Fig. 8.

9. These two sketches show the arms of the dancer who aims at fragility, but only achieves a painfully brittle appearance.
10. The same type of gesture performed more softly, and with the elbows supported.
11. *The dancer with long arms.* (A) This girl has decided that long arms are an asset and is making no attempt to control them. (B) An attempt to make the arms appear shorter by hunching the shoulders and bending the wrists and elbows. (C) This girl has

Lucile Grahn in "Eoline, ou la Dryade."

Carlotta Grisi in "La Péri."
(Circa 1840 — from contemporary lithographs)

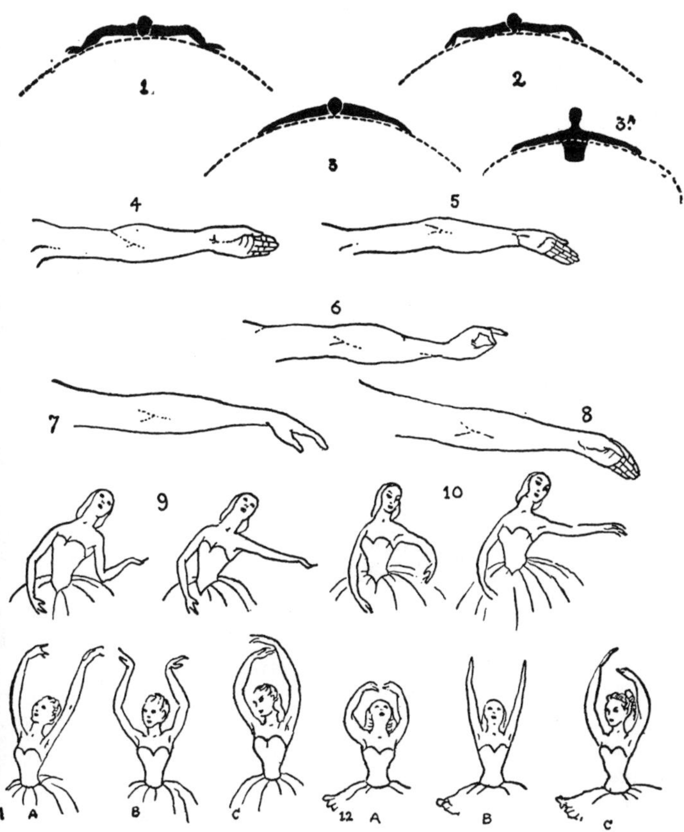

attended to her movements and to her whole appearance. Her arms have been trained so that their length is unnoticeable and their apparent shape greatly improved.

12. *The dancer with short arms.* (A) This dancer is determined to do a correct 5th position *en haut*, without even considering her general appearance. (B) This one's idea is to use every inch of her arms, hands, and fingers on all occasions; thus she draws attention to the shortness of her arms, by continual repetition. (C) This one knows that her arms should not be rounded as in Fig. A, nor extended as in B; but her carefully trained elbows and hands, her poise, and her joy in movement distract the spectator from studying her proportions.

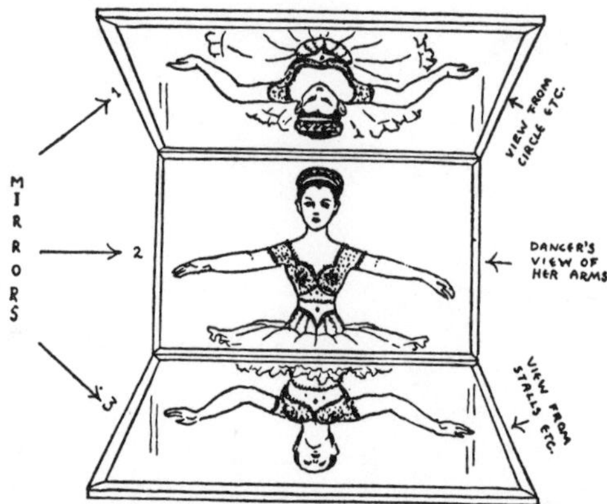

iv. Arms and the mirror

The fanciful arrangement of mirrors above shows that moral reflections are necessary to the dancer, as well as physical ones in the looking-glass. The reflection in mirror no. 2 shows a beginner regarding her arms; she sees that they look quite smoothly disposed in a good second position. Nevertheless, the reflections in mirrors 1 and 3, which show the dancer respectively from above and below, prove that her elbows and wrists are "broken"; all her movements will look mean and cramped, and on the stage she will certainly have no grace.

The sketches below show one of the countless aspects of the use of the arms in movement. The broken lines show the actual compass of the leap, as described by the feet, and the dotted lines follow the course and direction of the arms. The man in sketch A has let his head and shoulders take care of themselves; the effect of his leap is restricted to the actual distance he can cover. The man in sketch B has studied the placing of his head, shoulders, and arms, and his leap will only seem to end when he pleases to relax his pose; the movement being carried on by the direction of his arms, etc. (indicated by arrows), even after he has landed. All steps of elevation can be infinitely improved, and made either soft or brilliant, in this manner.

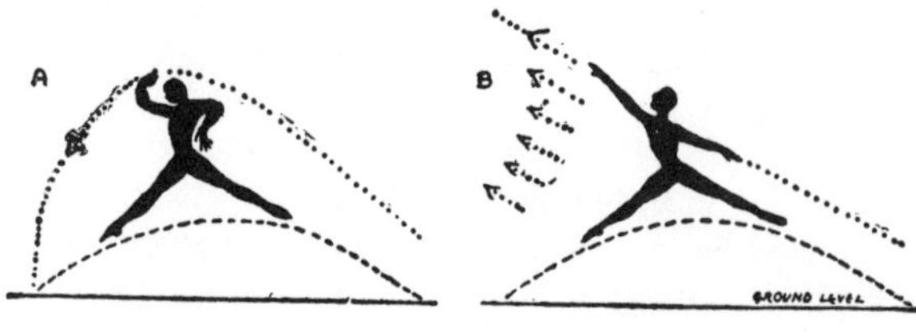

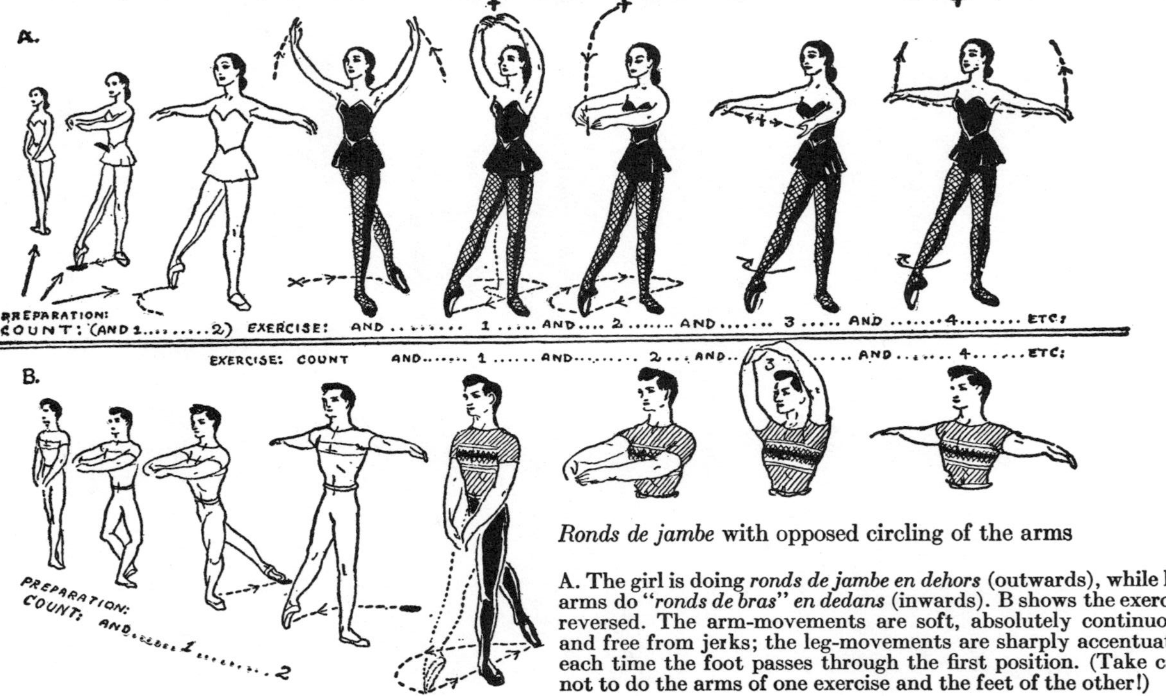

Ronds de jambe with opposed circling of the arms

A. The girl is doing *ronds de jambe en dehors* (outwards), while her arms do "*ronds de bras*" *en dedans* (inwards). B shows the exercise reversed. The arm-movements are soft, absolutely continuous, and free from jerks; the leg-movements are sharply accentuated each time the foot passes through the first position. (Take care not to do the arms of one exercise and the feet of the other!)

CHAPTER III. ON PRACTICAL SCIENCE

I. *Explanation*

The practical science of dancing is a subject that needs to be approached with extreme caution. Most of us associate the word *science* with the driest of hard facts, but this association is probably due to an uninspired science-master in our early youth. There is a science pertaining to every art—the science of diagnosing those elements which can be codified and passed on to others. If the resulting lesson is found dull, the fault is not in the art in question, but in the unsuitability of either the teacher or the pupil.

In dancing, in addition to the purely physical and mechanical side (which is examined briefly in Chapter I), there is a whole science that covers the practicability of imparting to an audience the emotions which we all experience, but which can only be articulated by the art of movement. It is at this point that dancing becomes an art, for without the means of displaying these emotions, the dancer performs only for his own benefit; therefore, if he is the victim of certain technical limitations and has not the skill with which to convey all the human passions to the spectator, the deepest of his feelings will remain unrevealed, and his work will be lifeless and uninteresting.

Today there is a marked tendency to confuse the purely mechanical aspect of dancing with the more intelligent, scientific aspect. While the mechanics of dancing may be said to concern the actual mastery of one's body, this cannot be fully achieved without scientific study, which concerns the full use of that mastery—that is, its suitable display and control.

If you confine yourself exclusively to the study of the mechanical side of dancing, you are likely to lose all sense of logic. Your legs may become marvelously "turned out," but it is probable that you will never realize the purpose of this convention; whereas a fencer or a boxer would tell you that turned-out feet make it possible to take a quick step in any direction and to maintain the balance at the same time. If you develop a great elevation and also thick ankles, how are you going to discover that unless you drop your heels to the ground at the conclusion of each leap, your ankles will get thicker and thicker?

In the remaining pages of this chapter I have tried to indicate the general application of science to movement by a very few practical examples.

II. *Notes on Balance: i. in adage*

Sketch A: with the leg raised *à la 4e en avant*, lean forward very slightly. If you try too hard to "tuck your tail in," you will achieve position B. C, *à la 2e:* be careful to retract the hip of the working leg, or else—see D. E, *à la 4e derrière:* here your back is most important. Don't attempt to lift your leg higher than is possible with the back strongly supported, or—see F. *Hint for maintaining the balance in these positions in adage:* the dotted lines represent pieces of string, imagined by the dancer, holding his knee to his waist.

Good equilibrium depends largely on a properly supported back. G: improperly held arms in this 5th position cause an undue arching of the back. H: an improved position. I: rising on *pointes* throws the girl's weight forward; to counteract this, she leans backwards, causing a deportment that is ugly and harmful to the physique. J: the same girl, having applied the rules for deportment on p. 19.

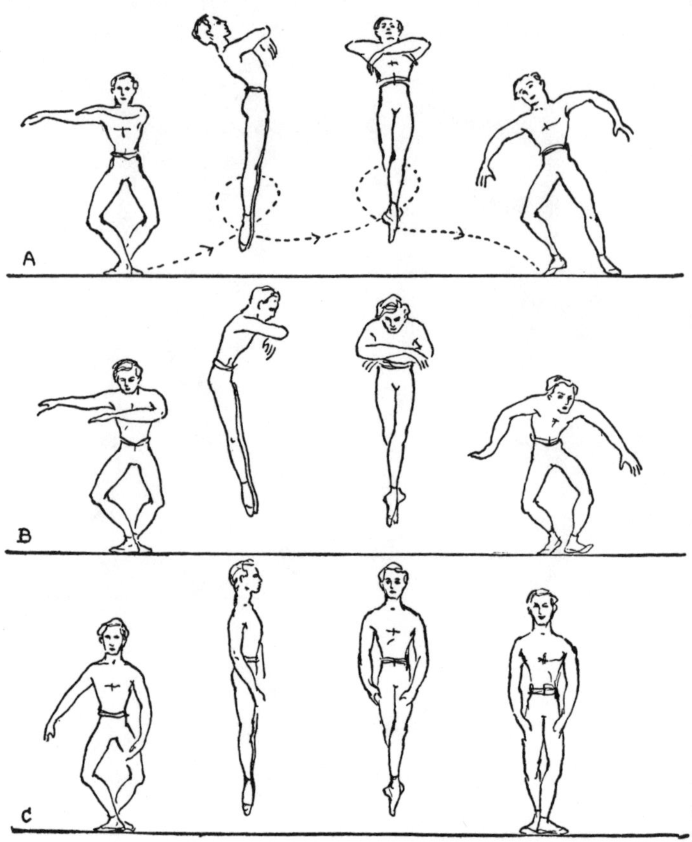

Notes on Balance: ii. in doubles tours

A number of students find great difficulty in performing double turns in the air, even when admirable physique is in their favor. Losing the balance at the conclusion of the step is the most common cause of this failure, and above are two reasonable explanations.

A: If you hold your arms as high as this, you will probably overbalance backwards when you land. B: If you try to counteract this by holding the arms a little lower and leaning forward, you are likely to fall on your face. C: The safest method is to hold the arms *à demi.*

The use of the Head in Turning

In some forms of turning, the head can remain facing the dancer's front, as in the double turns shown on the left; or it can move so that the face always seems to be presented to the audience, by a rapid movement of the head from shoulder to shoulder, as shown in fig. 1, above. Here the dancer (who is perhaps performing a series of diagonal turns) chooses a spot to look at, preferably at the back of the stalls; this spot is represented above by the mark on the placard.

2. The head can lead a turn, as it does in this *tour en renversé en dedans.* (Compare with the head-movement on pp. 42–3: *renversé en dehors.*)

3. *Fouettés.* Sketch C is a view of a *fouetté* accorded to the audience by many dancers who perform this step perfectly. A possible reason is advanced by the accompanying diagram, A, B, and a possible solution on the one below, D, E. F shows the correct view of a *fouetté.* The mistaken version is largely committed by the dancer who is technically overtrained, but who has no knowledge of the laws of stage perspective, which is dealt with in the succeeding chapter.

III. *Notes on Elevation*

Nos. 1, 2, and 3 above show a *sissone en arrière*, performed with virility and enthusiasm. The deep *plié* (1) throws the dancer far into the air. Nos. 4, 5, and 6 show a version of the same *sissone* performed with a half-hearted *plié*. 8: when performing steps of elevation such as *entrechats*, remember that a plane is helped by its wings, and hold the arms slightly away from the body. (Remember, too, that a plane's wings do not flap.) The arms held as in no. 7 conceal the contours of the body and do nothing to help your elevation. *On right:* adjustment of BALANCE IN ACTION. Balance in dancing is not simply a matter of avoiding a fall: in ballet, equilibrium should be used to its fullest extent. In sketches A, 1–7, the girl is performing a *developpé à la 4e devant* (1–4), then a *posé* (5–6) into an *attitude devant* (7). The pleasing *abandon* of fig. 7 is due to the sweeping movement of the *posé* (4–6). Sketches B, 4–7, correspond with the similarly numbered sketches of A above, and show the way in which a final attitude is prejudiced by a "mean" *posé* (B, 4–5). C, 1, shows an arabesque after an inadequate *posé;* C, 2, after a good big step forward.

A
1
2
3
4
5
6
7
(Compare with similarly numbered sketches above.)
B
4
5
6
7
C
1
2

CHAPTER IV. ON PHYSICAL AND STAGE PERSPECTIVES

i. Explanation

It is the purpose of this chapter to introduce the subject of stage perspective, which concerns the dancer's relation to his audience. Space is limited, but if the reader feels that he has grasped the meaning of the chapter, he will be in a position to work out the details for himself.

When we go to a play, we may find that an inexperienced actor is continually inaudible because he turns his back to the audience without realizing that when he does so, he should raise his voice. On this occasion it is quite easy for the spectator to perceive what is wrong with the actor's performance. In the performance of ballet exactly the same critical principles may be applied—except that instead of audibility, degrees of visibility become the most important consideration; and any faults of this nature are far more difficult to diagnose. The additional complications of music, libretto, *décor*, and choreographic design all tend to obscure individual shortcomings, which may be ruining the production. Indeed, lack of stage perspective causes a bad performance more often than lack of technical skill.

Stage perspective may conveniently be divided into two categories: (i) *physical perspective*, or the view of himself which the *soliste* consciously displays to his audience; (ii) *stage perspective*, or the view displayed by the dancers who are taking part in some general choreographic scheme.

There are certain rules governing the view of himself which a dancer displays to his *maître-de-ballet*. These, however, do not prepare the dancer adequately for theatrical performance unless the teacher insists that his pupil be perpetually conscious of an imaginary auditorium throughout his entire training. Although nothing can replace actual

ABOVE: THE EIGHT DIRECTIONS OF THE BODY.

experience of stage and auditorium, yet an exacting teacher who can give demonstrations and criticisms can do much to prepare his pupil for his professional debut. Thus the intensely difficult art of self-visualization becomes second nature to the dancer.

At the base of these two pages are sketches of the *eight directions of the body*. They are a Cecchetti exercise, and are a study in perspective, as well as in *adage*. The importance of the *directions* of the body, as a study in balance, weight-adjustment, nobility and grace of carriage, is usually appreciated by the dancer and his teacher; care is often taken to present the correct angle of each pose; but the main object of this exercise tends to become overlooked, in that the dancer of today often fails to apply the precepts of the *eight directions* to all other movements in dancing.

Herein lies one of the principal reasons that cause a dancer who gives a brilliant technical performance in class to disappoint us on the stage; conversely, here lies the reason whereby the dancer who has only moderate technical capabilities but a highly developed instinct for self-visualization can employ this sense on the stage to bewitch us into believing he has performed technical feats far out of his reach. (How often have you heard a dancer's success hailed with the comment: "—but he can't do a *thing* in class!")

Very few people are born already equipped with an instinctive feeling for stage perspective; and very few teachers and dancers concern themselves with the subject, which is closely akin to good showmanship, and therefore probably considered slightly vulgar. Nevertheless, the perpetual back views and distortions accorded by the dancer of today to his audience are as unprofessional as they are contrary to the traditions of stage etiquette.

ii. Practical perspective

One of the greatest difficulties to be solved in the training of a ballet student is to find a method by which he can be taught to understand the adaptation of classroom technique to that of a stage performance. In the classroom he faces his teacher, who usually tells him that similarly on the stage he must "keep his face to the audience." This injunction generally constitutes the student's entire training in stagecraft.

Clearly this is quite inadequate, and at the foot of the page is the Cecchetti solution to the problem. The square in the upper part of the sketch is a diagram of the "Cecchetti stage"; the lower sketch shows the same stage put to fanciful use. The classroom floor is treated in just the same way; the pupils memorize the direction numbers, 1–8. If the teacher says: "Stand facing 5, turn your head to 2," the pupil stands facing the teacher and turns his head to his left. The center of the classroom and center of the stage are always borne in mind; for the *soliste* who makes a bad guess at the exact middle of the stage will spoil his *variation*, cause his poses to seem off balance, and give the audience the impression that they are seeing only half a performance.

N.B. The eight directions of the body, the terms *effacée* and *croisée*, the open and closed positions of the feet, etc., are technical designations that always remain the same, whichever way the demonstrator is facing. If you were in the position *croisée devant*, for example (see sketch on p. 36), and the stage revolved with you on it, you would be *croisée devant* the whole way round. All exceptions to the rules of physical and stage perspectives come under the category of *choreographic fantasy;* and it is only through a thorough knowledge of the basic rules of perspective that a choreographer's wishes and intentions can be effectively and intelligently carried out.

The sketches 1–4, above and below, relate to the drawings of a detail from the Mazurka in *Les Sylphides*, shown on the two succeeding pages. Fig. 1 shows the conclusion of a *grand jeté en tournant*, as we often see it today. This view of a dancer, at such a moment, is by no means confined to performances of *Les Sylphides;* but as this ballet fails completely when each moment is not carefully studied, it is easily understood that lack of stage perspective is sure to cause an unsuccessful performance. Fig. 2 could have a place as a pose in a ballet—but not when it indicates failure to "get round" after the *grand jeté*, at the same time spoiling the beautiful pose that succeeds it (sketch E overleaf). The diagrams 3 and 4 show the visual difference between the incorrect position, 1 above, and the correct position, A overleaf.

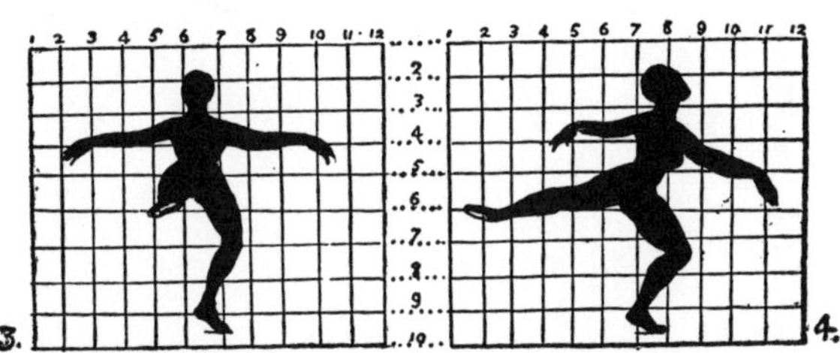

iii. A detail from the Mazurka, in "Les Sylphides"

The sketches on these pages show an excerpt from the Mazurka in *Les Sylphides*, beginning with the conclusion of a *grand jeté en tournant*. This movement directly succeeds the sequence shown on pp. 54–5, in the chapter "On Music and the Dancer." The demonstrator is the same.

Les Sylphides is a ballet of incomparable beauty, but it cannot be performed with success unless the dancers possess unusual interpretative powers. Present-day performances—one cannot say "interpretations"—leave the newcomer **in**

pardonable doubt as to the cause of the widespread enthusiasm occasioned by the original production; ballet veterans quite simply never want to see it again. A great deal of criticism has been leveled at the dancers, on the score of insufficient poetic feeling and other grounds; but when we remind ourselves that even a poet cannot function unless he has a certain mastery over his own language, we realize that a dancer cannot give a poetic interpretation of a role when he has not been trained either musically or with regard to the elements of stage perspective.

The delicacy of the poses A and D would be lost if addressed to the backcloth. If the pose in sketch 2 on page 39 be substituted for D, then sketch E, on the right, becomes a sorry spin-cum-scramble instead of the lovely attitude shown here. (Compare with direction *croisée derrière* on p. 37.)

The small sketches, B and C, show the transitional steps, so that anyone who wishes to scrutinize or essay this particular sequence may do so. It would be well to note that the demonstrator was able to give a detailed account, not only of each pose, but of each intermediary movement in slow motion, and also to provide an excellent practical reason for each one.

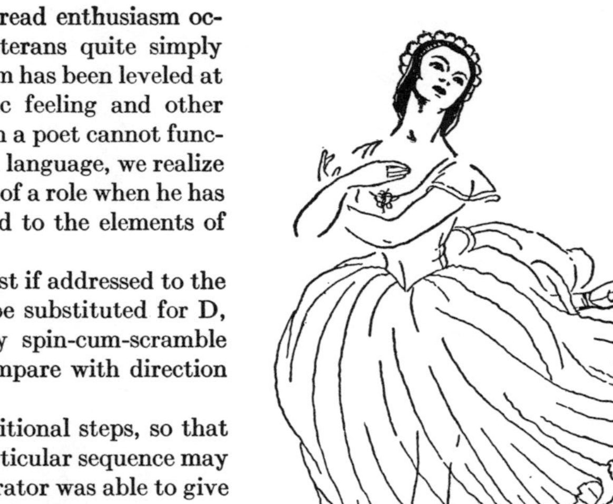

N.B. The sketches on these pages, and throughout the book, are not intended to represent inflexible rules, but are to be taken as examples from which the reader can form judgments, rules, and substitutions of his own. (For further observations on *Perspective*, see Chapter VII, "On Partnering.")

iv. Tour en renversé en dehors.

Here are two versions of *renversés en dehors*, the one above being notable for its flowing movements, and the one below for stylization of the *renversé* character of the head. When the reader bears in mind that these turns must be performed in about two to three seconds, and that the value of either will be lost if any of the movements are "faked" or *performed at the wrong angle to the spectator*, he will understand that a knowledge of perspective must be second nature to the dancer. There is no time for reflection.

CHAPTER V. ON "LINE"

i. Explanation

The first purpose of this chapter is to disabuse the reader of the idea that a "good *line*" and a "good *arabesque*" signify the same thing. Let us examine the reasons that have given rise to this confusion.

The primary cause is associative. An *arabesque* is a pose that is easily recognized, and one with which the ballet-lover and the student of ballet first become familiar. Consequently the student, hearing constantly linked references to *line* and *arabesque*, draws the inevitable inference: viz., that a dancer who has a "beautiful line" must have a "high *arabesque*" (see fig. 8), and this misconception has now been communicated to the lover of ballet as well.

In reality, a sense of *line* is not achieved by acrobatic means, but is a feeling for physical harmony, which should form a never absent part of the dancer's sensibility, and which he should be able to adjust to every aspect of dancing, whether academic, romantic, dramatic, rhythmic, or characteristic. Even a dancer who has an unpleasing *arabesque* (perhaps for physical reasons) may quite possibly possess good *line* in movement, which the possessor of a "high arabesque" would do well to study.

As *line* relates to every posture in dancing, so it relates to all movements in dancing. A dancer who has studied the *line* of each pose, but has failed to apply the same principles to the movements that link the poses together, is not a dancer at all. His work may be compared to the conversation of a parrot, whose meaningless and discordant babble is occasionally relieved by a recognizable word or phrase, which have, however, no relation to one another.

Although the two terms are not synonymous, it is obvious that the principles which govern the use of *line* should also be applied to *arabesques*. A brief portrayal of the generally accepted rules appears at the head of the opposite page.

The word *arabesque* is derived from the name of a form of Moorish ornament, in which the use of curves, and of the diagonal line, will be noticed (fig. 1). Musically, the term conveys a form of melodic ornamentation of a somewhat voluptuous nature. Hence, geometrically speaking, the formation of a right angle, which is produced by raising the leg in a line with the hip while keeping the body upright, has little apparent relation to the implication of the word *arabesque*, which suggests a certain flowing quality, and which the "pin man" (fig. 2) does

not possess, in spite of the fact that *his pose is technically correct.* This pose should be practiced by the dancer who is interested in controlling his body, so that his *line* can be modified according to his personal taste and not restricted by physical limitations.

According to the opinion most general among teachers of taste, the *line* of an *arabesque* should run unbroken from the fingers of the higher arm, through the body, to the toe of the extended leg. (See figs. 3–6.) Although the back must be supported and made as straight as possible, a slight curve in the body is dictated by nature, and therefore makes the *line* at once more pliable and graceful.

The supporting leg, whether straight or bent, serves as a sort of pivot, like the center of a pair of scales; and, whatever angles are employed, the *line* itself should remain the same.

The sketches on this page show: fig. 1, part of a Moorish arabesque; 2, the theoretical position for a *first arabesque;* 3–6, a simplified version of the use of *line* in various *arabesques*, the course of which is emphasized by dots. Fig. 7; a spineless caricature of fig. 2; this familiar example of an *arabesque* shows that the entire purpose of the pose has been overlooked. 8, another familiar distortion of an arabesque, which is usually described as "doing the splits on one leg."

ii. Interpretation

"*The movements of the soul . . . cannot be limited to a fixed number of gestures.*" Thus Noverre addresses all those who would try to make a rule of thumb for all postures in dancing; heaven knows in what contempt he would have held that school of thought which would limit *line* in dancing solely to the execution of *arabesques*!

The drawing below shows Mlle Spessivtzewa as Giselle. Here is a wonderful use of *line*. It is apparently simple—so nearly straight from brow to toe—but in the course of that line the whole feeling of this romantic ballet is so subtly conveyed that we may be taken in by the gentle relaxation of this superlative artist. Anything further removed from a "high *arabesque*" would be hard to find; it is an excellent example of *interpretative dancing*, in which *line* allied to feeling plays an indispensable part, and without which ballets such as the second act of *Giselle* and *Les Sylphides* virtually cease to exist.

(from a contemporary photograph.)

This drawing of Mlle Pavlova as the Dragonfly is another outstanding example of the combination of *line* and feeling. This pose is as vivacious and skillful as the other is nostalgic and restrained; *abandon* and melancholy, both are equally effective, and are the result of the same artistry.

Below: Sketch A shows an insensitive pose with no *line* at all, the feeling displayed being more indicative of indigestion than romance. This position resembles a propped-up picture-frame (B), whereas Spessivtzewa's interpretation can best be compared with the work of nature (C). D shows a muddled version of Pavlova's pose; purposeless, and with that familiar view of underneath the chin, it resembles a shapeless parcel (E). F shows a floral equivalent for Pavlova's pose.

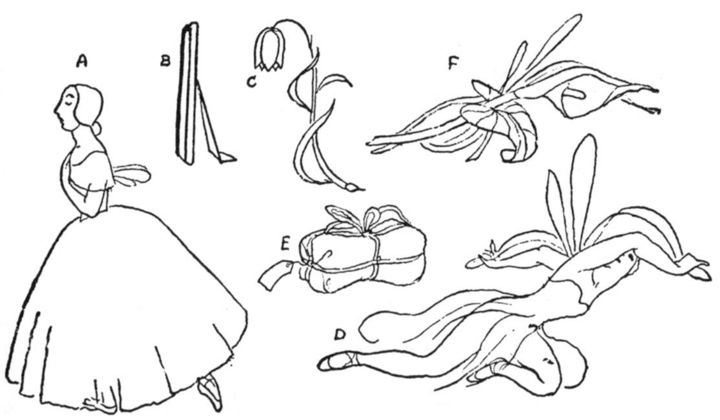

iii. Misinterpretation: an Ugly Duckling?

"A dancer who has studied the *line* of each pose, but has failed to apply the same principles to the movements that link the poses together, is not a dancer at all"—certainly not a ballerina. The girl in the sketches has all the physical advantages she needs; she is practicing her *adage* with two friends. (While the above excerpt from *Swan Lake* is not entirely accurate, it is sufficiently typical of classical *adage* to serve its purpose, which is to emphasize a type of faulty intermediary movement.)

Start examining the sketches at the top of the right-hand page. Fig. 1, a well-placed *arabesque* supported by the Prince; 2, she leaves the Prince; so far, so good. She is going to do a *posé*, and fig. 3 shows her as she decides where she will put her foot; her preoccupation is shown by her face and posture. In fig. 4 she has forgotten she is a

princess, or a ballerina, or half a swan. With an unnecessarily high *développé*, hunched shoulders, and posterior to match, she makes an ungainly prelude to the appealing *arabesque* that follows (fig. 5).—In this case, it is doubtful whether she could hold this low *arabesque* without the aid of the Prince's friend; after her enormous *développé*, unaided she would probably land flat on her face.

As she leaves the Prince's friend, it is her dread that the Prince's hand will be out of reach for her coming *arabesque penché*. She pivots on her heels (figs. 6–7), while expressions ranging from acute anxiety to heartfelt relief succeed one another on her face. Fig. 8: with the *arabesque penché* she turns into a princess again, but only temporarily; for fig. 9 shows a moment that should never occur, but will take place unless dancers watch their *line in movement;* the Prince and the Princess, face to face, on bent knees, en route for their next pose.

CHAPTER VI. ON MUSIC AND THE DANCER

i. Definition

The question of the musicality of a dancer is often the subject for discussion, but a definition of the matter is seldom attempted. Consequently many of the discussions are conducted at cross-purposes. In the following pages the subject is introduced briefly, in its relation to present-day ballet; there is not sufficient space to discuss all objections and exceptions, and the reader must supply these controversial pros and cons himself.

In the eighteenth century, in his *Letters* on dancing, Noverre directs some well-aimed missiles at the unmusical dancer of his day. We can scarcely do better than quote one passage here:

"*There are ears that remain out of time with, and insensible to, the most striking music; there are a lesser number of them that feel the time, but cannot seize upon its niceties; lastly, there are others that appreciate naturally and easily the most difficult melodies. Mlle Camargo and M. Lany enjoyed that precious gift and that precision which accord to dancing a spirit of vivacity and gaiety that is never found in those dancers who have less sensitiveness and delicacy of hearing . . . a dancer can have very delicate feeling and not reveal it to the spectator, if he does not possess the art of using with ease the tendons by which the instep is used.*"

One of the most interesting points contained in the above extract is the nature of the reference to Camargo. It is generally known that she was a great dancer, but her artistic gifts have become somewhat obscured by her fame as the *danseuse* who shortened her skirts and scandalized the contemporary Grundys with a glimpse of twinkling ankles. Noverre, however, singles her out for her remarkable musicality.

A sixteenth-century poet named Marino, in his poem *Adonis*, described the dance of Terpsichore, in the course of which he alludes to the execution of *pirouettes*, beats, *entrechats*, *arabesques*, etc., in the most exact manner, by describing the movements themselves, and without, of course, using our technical terminology. At the outset of the stanza he says: "*Her attention is fixed on the harmonious sounds, while she arranges her steps in prelude. . . . Marking each note, minding every pause, promptly she obeys each phrase of the music, which she respects as mistress of every motion.*"

A dancer famed for his musicality was Carlo Blasis. In his book *The Code of Terpsichore* (1830) he describes how he used to induce his father to extemporize on the pianoforte while he himself "*endeavored to follow his musical intentions.*" He was given this idea by the celebrated dancer M. Gardel, who said that the equally famous M. Dupré used thus to "*accustom his ear to catch measures and rhythms*" with greater rapidity.

From these extracts and quotations, it will be seen that in every century dancers, and in particular choreographers, have been deeply concerned with the relation of music to dancing. In its primitive form the question of musical relationship was that of making most of the music oneself, by the means of clapping, stamping, and singing. Now that the study of bodily movement has been allowed to become separated from the study of music, the relationship between movement and music has grown increasingly underestimated.

Imagine a band of primitives conducting a burial ceremony with songs and dances. They do not need to be told that their expressions must range from solemnity to anguish, that their gestures must be chastened and slow, and that they must keep time to the rhythms of their songs; for each one knows the music and its meaning backwards, and he is also well acquainted with the melancholy character of the ceremony. Compare this example with the various musical-dramatic moments in the stage invention *Giselle*, and examine the faces and gestures of the gathering on these occasions. The great gulf formed by civilization, which divides these two examples of music and movement, should be bridged by art, and trodden by Terpsichore.

In the normal ballet classroom the student's musical training consists in being told to "keep time to the music." That is to say, he is taught to understand that music is divided into bars,

Marie CAMARGO 1710-1770.
(from the painting by Nicolas Lancret)

some of which contain two beats, others three, four, or six beats, and so on; if he can always remain "on the beat," he is considered musical; if he can still recognize the beat even during the usual orchestral fluctuations of timing, he is accounted very musical indeed.

The trouble starts when we realize that music contains more than bars and beats. Even if a dancer can hold his pose for exactly the same duration as one of the instrumentalists holds his note, it does not follow that therefore the dancer is musical. Music is made up of phrases, and tone, as well as of time, and together these elements give music its power to move us to corresponding emotions ourselves. This is the very substance of music, and may be termed the *emotional content.*

If a dancer is trained without continual reference to this emotional content, the result is that he develops a "deaf ear" for tone and phrasing; he disregards the obvious melodic message and the feeling of the music in order to decipher and to display to the spectator his ability to recognize the number of beats in a bar under any circumstances.

It is well known that many people who have not the least technical knowledge of music, nor any melodic or rhythmic sense themselves, can yet be profoundly moved by the various musical colors and moods. Hearing emotional music, and confronted by a dancer who is apparently unaffected by emotion, such a person will probably condemn the dancer as a "cold" performer. What he means is that the dancer is not in accompaniment with the music. Any number of brilliant steps, matchless technique, the correct number of beats in a bar—all are of no avail. The dancer may be performing at the same time as, and in time with, the music, but he is not interpreting it if he is emotionally unresponsive.

It has been affirmed that it is sufficient to teach a dancer to "keep time" during his student days, and that musical interpretation, as already described, is in the province of the choreographer. Undeniably, it is the first consideration of the choreographer to see that his ballets, and all who take part in them, are one with the music; but to present him with a group of performers who know something of "time" and nothing whatever of tone and phrasing is to ask him, musically speaking, to educate his own dancers in the short space of time allowed for the rehearsal of a ballet. This he will try to do; but what a waste of his time, and how disheartening, to struggle to describe feelings, impulses, and shades of atmosphere that cannot be put into words, but only shown in movement, by a capable exponent!

The choreographer is an artist—that is, one of those people who get ideas from the thin air—and he relies on dancers to bring those ideas to life. Therefore it is easily understood that the consummation of his ideas must be limited by the dancers' own limitations.

It is said that those who are born already able to swim find it difficult to teach others to do so. For the same reason, those who have been born with a highly developed musical sensitivity find it difficult to appreciate the problems of those who are not similarly gifted. This musical dilemma would be greatly reduced if exercises could be arranged that feature the interpretation of different pieces of music which are of the same *time*, but of *various moods and emotional content.* In this way dancers would learn to respond to this intangible but powerful element in music; and choreographers would gain greater inspiration from watching classes, as well as increased co-operation from the dancers.

When the dancer is one with the music, it is immaterial whether he is following the music, or whether the music is following him. When the harmony between the respective movements in dancing and music is complete, the result is so compelling that it will captivate even the most unmusical spectator.

In these pages I have done my best to describe the quality of musicality in words; on the two following pages, I have attempted to clarify the matter a little further, with the help of sketches.

The sketches are based on part of Fokine's ballet, *Les Sylphides;* since this work is referred to so frequently in this book, here is a sketch of Marie Taglioni as La Sylphide, in which role she first introduced the romantic *tutu* as adapted for *Les Sylphides.*

Marie Taglioni as "La Sylphide:" 1832.

(from a contemporary lithograph.)

A.
EDGE OF STAGE
B.
C.
X
(A. AGAIN)
X
(A. AGAIN)
Meno mosso
KEY TO SKETCHES: A—B........A—C.......A—D.................E...
p sostenuto
f (grand jeté en tournant......;

"Les Sylphides"—a detail from the Mazurka

The sketches on these pages show an example of the musical interpretation of the accompanying bars of music. The usual demonstration consists, approximately, in three repetitions of sketches A and C, which shows a disregard for the instructions *p* and *f*—that is, *piano*, inscribed under bar A–B, which grows to *forte* (bar E).

Sketch E is the preparation for the *grand jeté en tournant*, which figures in the chapter on *stage perspective* (pp. 40–1).

The interpretation selected, and shown here, is that of Celia Franca. Naturally musical, she has also made a serious study of music; which means that while a musical interpretation is second nature to her, she is fully conscious of all she does.

A dancer who has had a musical training *as part of ballet training* is sufficiently rare to be remarkable.

For further reference to musicality in relation to several dancers, see Chapter VII, p. 61, "On Partnering," where team-work is briefly discussed.

iii. The Rhythmical Dancer

In the first part of this chapter we have examined briefly the meaning of the term *musical* when used in conjunction with the ballet-dancer. We have seen that the genuinely musical dancer has interpretative powers which can reveal to us all facets and qualities of the music, whether they be lyrical or staccato, emotional or academic, with complete accuracy and timing.

Under the heading of musicality a small group of dancers stands out with startling clarity; the members of this group are the *rhythmical dancers*. As this chapter would be incomplete unless some tribute were paid to them, here it is, in the form of an analysis.

We can begin by affirming that the rhythmical dancer senses musical tempi with such ease that he can afford to "play with the time"; in the words of Mr. Percy Scholes, in his notes on *good rhythm in performance*, "such slight but purposeful departures from regularity suggest life as opposed to mechanism."

It is these "departures from regularity"—slight anticipations of the beat, infinitesimal lingerings after it—that provide us with a feeling of excitement and satisfaction. We sense that the dancer is using every part of his body to make the musical rhythms spring to visible life, that he has exchanged his very heartbeats for the pulsation of the music; we have complete confidence that the dancer will only quarrel with the time of the music for some purpose of his own. He is incapable of offending our sense of time, but never tires of pretending he is about to do so; hence the excitement.

Such rhythm, when possessed by a dancer to a marked degree, is an attribute that is as forceful as it is instinctive. The supreme judgment and conviction of a rhythmical dancer cannot be acquired; but it is a most stimulating quality, particularly when used consciously to gain a certain effect.

It would be natural to assume that the superlatively rhythmical dancer cannot use his special gifts choreographically, as it is obviously impossible to teach a company of dancers to execute steps in this highly personal manner; thus one might logically suppose that the rhythmical dancer must remain an inspiring *soliste*. Fortunately, this is not so; choreography is not a matter of the multiplication of scores of small ideas, but rather the art of suggesting details by the means of a general scheme. Thus the rhythmical dancer can codify certain elements in his own performance, which can be taught to most dancers and can become in this way a highly personal form of choreography.

Of all those who have succeeded in work of this genre, the ballets of Léonide Massine and of Walter Gore (once his pupil) are the most remarkable. The work of Jerome Robbins, a new choreographer, whets the appetite by displaying the same mastery of rhythm.

Noverre, writing on music, remarks on the acute sense of rhythm and timing displayed by the people of whole provinces in Germany. "This natural and innate taste for music brings in its train a similar liking for dancing. . . . Counterpoint, which is undoubtedly the touchstone of the most delicate ear, presents the least difficulty to them. . . ." One wonders what would have happened to that countryside gusto for rhythm if it were subjected to the average ballet-dancer's training of today. Would it survive?

Nowadays the most remarkable exponents of an innate sense of rhythm of an astonishing quality are the Negroes, whom we see all too seldom on the stage. Singular rhythmical dancing is still practiced by Spanish villagers, but La Argentina, who showed their very soul all over the world, dances no more. Perhaps the highest standard of natural rhythm, as described on this page, is to be seen in the largest *palais de danse* in the big towns, where love of rhythm is still the reason that causes the strangest mixture of people to go there and dance. And perhaps—who knows?—visits to these dancing-palaces would keep alive in ballet-dancers that vivacious, careless, and prompt reaction to basic musical rhythms of which their present-day training tends to deprive them.

CHAPTER VII. ON PARTNERING

PARTNERING & PERSPECTIVE: for explanation see overleaf.
4
5
6
1st lift
10
11
12
2nd lift
for 14 and 15 repeat sketches 2 and 3
16
17
3rd lift

i. Preliminary note on perspective in partnering

[ILLUSTRATED ON PAGES 58–9]

The sketches that relate to the chapter on *perspective* (p. 36) are nos. 5, 11, and 17, as these are three lifts that show a certain use of perspective in choreography.

On p. 39, fig. 1, the dancer who presents a confused and negative view of herself to the spectator, with her leg pointing directly at him, has been used to show a faulty stage sense. Here, in nos. 5 and 11, the girl is in a somewhat similar posture, with her leg pointed at the audience, her face hidden by her arm, and most of her torso—and her partner—hidden by quantities of billowing tarlatan. In this case the two lifts, 5 and 11, are part of a choreographic scheme designed to build up the *pas-de-deux* to an effective finale, which is achieved as shown by sketch 17, where the same lift is performed for the third time—but on this occasion the dancer travels sideways, thus displaying the most beautiful view of the lift to the audience.

ii. Practical observations

The three lifts by themselves are sufficient to illustrate the point described above; the series of sketches has been completed, however, including the main transitional movements, in order to illustrate some notes on partnering.

From a careful study of the sketches, it will be seen that the girl and the man are *dancing together*. That is to say, in the time which it takes to perform this musical extract (say approximately fifteen seconds), there are a number of occasions when the pair might bang their heads together, miss a lift by being too far apart, trip each other; and many more occasions when they might simply look ungainly. For instance, take nos. 10, 11, and 12, which show an awkward forward lift, face to face; unless there is complete co-operation here, the two dancers will find themselves in a most unbecoming and precarious posture, beginning and ending with a general scramble.

Perhaps it is worth adding that in each of the lifts the man has to walk a few steps with the girl lifted. If she tries to travel herself, instead of leaping straight upwards and leaving her partner to propel her through the air, either she will throw the man completely off his balance, or else she will find herself leaping alone, while the man runs after her, vainly trying to catch her waist. Further awkward moments will occur throughout any *pas-de-deux* if the man rises on his toes when he lifts his partner. She will feel utterly insecure, as the man on his points will certainly rock unsteadily backwards and forwards.

The handsome and graceful partner of traditional ballet, the *danseur noble*, is usually chosen for his technical powers and his appearance as a *soliste;* if he is also notable for manliness, the quality of chivalry will develop unaided as he learns the technicalities of partnering. There are pitfalls, however, for all types of *danseur noble*. The chivalrous and manly partner, in his zeal to help his ballerina to give a brilliant performance, sometimes overdoes things. For example, to assist her pirouettes he spins her like a top by her waist, supporting her all the time; this is exasperating for a ballerina who can spin perfectly well by herself. On the other hand, some *danseurs* leave their ballerina with the feeling that she hasn't a partner at all; this may be because he lacks experience, or because he is still virtually a *soliste*.

To be a good partner, whether male or female, is by no means a matter of technique alone. In the first act of the ballet *Giselle*, the encounters of the village maiden with her disguised lover, Count Albrecht, must range from the gay nonsense of a rustic courtship to the tragedy of Giselle's madness and death; neither the ballerina nor her partner can evoke the emotional atmosphere unaided, and between them they must make the old story live, and convince themselves and their audience that the laughter and tragedy are taking place for the first time. Albrecht's horror and remorse at the death of Giselle must prepare the audience for the nostalgic scene that follows in which the ghost of Giselle floats compassionately among the damp trees and tries to save her lover from the doom that awaits him. Those contemporary photographs which show Karsavina and Nijinsky as Giselle and Albrecht repay repeated study, for they retain an atmosphere of artistic unity that should inspire every modern dancer. (See sketch on p. 63.)

With regard to the team-work of a whole company: here every consideration applicable to the individual dancer must be subordinated to consideration of the performance as a whole. (In support of this statement, the reader has only to consider what would happen on a battlefield if each member of an army insisted on carrying out his own personal plan of campaign.) For example, take the case of a *pas-de-quatre* in which each dancer must perform identical steps; although each one may be equally musical, the general appearance of the four will be far from tidy unless they co-operate with one another; the angles of the limbs, the height of the leaps, must be agreed upon, and regularly practiced and adhered to. How many *ensembles* have been spoiled because one dancer jumps just a little higher than the others, and lands constantly out of time with his companions! Such a dancer must learn cheerfully to conserve his superior elevation for his solos.

CHAPTER VIII. ON CLASSIFICATION

i. *On the classification of Ballets*

This chapter is mainly concerned with the use of the two adjectives, *classical* and *romantic*, as these two designations are most familiar to the ballet-goer, and most often misused. Definitions of the various types of modern ballets can only be attempted in this book to illustrate certain other points; their present classification must be left to the ballet-magazine editor, and their ultimate value to the theater-going public.

The argument for our discussion is as follows: although the classical *tutu* is easily distinguishable from the romantic *tutu* (see p. 67), this costume cannot be regarded with safety as the sole indicator of the nature of the ballet in which it is employed; moreover, although the terms *classical* and *romantic* have a certain meaning when linked with the word *tutu*, when used in a more general sense their significance is far less clearly defined. To take a simple example, although *Les Sylphides* is perhaps the most well-known of all *romantic* ballets, yet it can also be described as *classical*, in the sense that it has earned its place among standard works of art and has become a classic.

A development of this situation is that when someone refers to a ballet as "one of the classics," it is often left open to doubt whether the ballet in question has a place in tradition, like *Petrouchka*, or whether the allusion is to the academic form of ballet technique such as that employed in *Swan Lake.*

The expression "classical ballet" has now come to have a meaning of its own; but when used loosely it leads to confusion and cross-purposes. For example, a "classical *pas-de-deux*" now means an exerpt from, let us say, *Aurora's Wedding;* but a *pas-de-deux* arranged with the exclusive use of the academic ballet technique may also be described as "a classical *pas-de-deux.*"

Therefore, to avoid further complications, it would be advisable to substitute the word *academic* for *classical* on all suitable occasions.

Academic ballet conveys the traditional development of pure technique. The complete mastery of it should enable the dancer to perform any feat demanded by any choreographer, modern or otherwise. Although every movement in the academic technique is rigidly controlled, its aim is not to limit the dancer, but to reward him with a physical and artistic freedom unheard of in other schools of movement.

Three famous ballets from the classical repertoire featuring the use of the academic technique are *Swan Lake*, *The Sleeping Princess*, and *Coppélia*. Examples of famous romantic ballets are *Giselle*, *Les Sylphides*, and *Carnaval*.

ii. On the classification of the Ballerina

In order to compare the different characteristics of ballerinas, perhaps the most reasonable method is to begin by studying two of the great traditional roles and the various gifts and qualities they demand of their performers.

The ballerina's solos in *Swan Lake* are composed of pure academic technique, and designed to display to the fullest degree the technical

Famous Partners. Tamara KARSAVINA & Vaslav NIJINSKY in "Giselle" (1910). From a contemporary photograph.

and authoritative capabilities of the Swan Princess, and not to evoke any particular mood or atmosphere; the latter is left to the designer of costume and *décor*. This means that if the ballerina cannot introduce any emotional content into her role, but can give a performance that is technically perfect, the sparkle of her faultless execution will be sufficient in itself, as it has an appeal and a fire of its own.

In the solos of *Giselle* the academic technique is employed once more, and is by no means easy to execute; but here it is used as a means to a romantic end. A Giselle who has only technique and no emotional capability is a theatrical and artistic atrocity.

Therefore, it will be seen that a successful Swan Princess is by no means whatsoever a potentially successful Giselle.

iii. On the classification of the Danseur

In Chapter I we have seen that, physically speaking, there are two main types of dancer: viz. (i) the *jarreté*, most suited to lyrical and academic roles; (ii) the *arqué*, who is brilliant and rhythmical. Very exceptional is the dancer who conforms to neither of these two categories. But it cannot be stressed too clearly that either type, if he is suitably intelligent, accomplished, and adjustable, should be able to give an interesting performance of the roles that are physically suited to his opposite.

Those dancers of the *jarreté* type, to whom are usually assigned the roles of the *danseurs nobles*, should be able to give a different, but stimulating interpretation of the most robust type of role usually entrusted to the *arqué* dancer, bringing to bear on his movements all his innate grace and fluidity, and intelligence and vivacity to his deportment.

The *arqué* dancer, when it is demanded that he should assume the role of *danseur noble*, usually surprises the spectator at the outset by his *attaque* and virility; secondly, his supreme control of his muscles and movements lends him an especial dignity, which quite atones for that more languid grace associated with the *jarreté* dancer.

iv. On General Classification

The desire to classify human beings is an excellent thing, in the right degree. To have a knowledge of ballet, and to enjoy a certain discrimination, one must be able to recognize the different types of performer. Such classification, however, can become a peril, and directly opposed to any artistic advancement, if wielded like a whip over a company of dancers.

The Illusion of Classical-Romantic Ballet

"'Tis impossible to describe that with the hand which never entered into the imagination." (Giovanni Pietro Bellori, 1664.) *Sketches A:* Prince Siegfried watches his lady turn into a swan, and fly away. *Scene B:* The picture Siegfried must evoke and convey to the audience. It is said that when Nijinsky drew near this imagined and enchanted lake, his nostrils dilated as though he was scenting the damp mists. *Scene C:* If Siegfried does not really follow with his eyes the flight of the bewitched swan, then this is the picture he is in danger of conveying to his audience—a typical backstage scene.

Under the latter circumstances a girl may find herself confined to a pigeonhole labeled "Classical and Technical Roles Only." In certain cases, it is obviously right that she should remain there (every aspiring Pavlova cannot be allowed to inflict on the public her version of *The Dying Swan*). Nevertheless, if that girl is intelligent, as well as a successful classical dancer, the odds are that she could acquit herself well in a dramatic role—and benefit from the experience. If, in spite of this latent ability, she is kept rigidly in her pigeonhole, "Classical Dancer Only," her best work will soon begin to flag and she will be an example of *art held tongue-tied by authority*, which is a sign of mediocrity in the direction of the company.

In conclusion, it may be affirmed that there are as many types of dancer as there are great dancers. Two human beings are never exactly alike in every respect, physical and moral; and we can only use similes with safety when describing the separate qualities of a dancer.

Thus, we can say that a young man has the rhythm of a Massine, that he is as light as a Nijinsky, and that he resembles such-and-such a dancer in physique; but if this young man has the makings of a great dancer, we shall—and ought to—find ourselves at a loss to say exactly what "type" he is. He is his own type, although he may model himself on a score of others. His magic is the magic of art: built on tradition, but ever original.

One genius can only be said to resemble another in that the other is a genius also.

Contemporary classical *tutu*: Galina Ulanova in *Swan Lake* (from a photograph.)

Contemporary Romantic *tutu*: costume for a *Wilis* in *Giselle* by Hugh Stevenson.

CHAPTER IX. ON STYLE AND CHARACTER

i. On style

Up to the present I have attempted certain analyses and definitions in these pages, and have discussed various components of ballet with the purpose of discovering how the dancer can rid himself of those limitations and misunderstandings which hamper his artistic and physical development and prevent him from enjoying that absolute freedom which is the artist's right. Now we come to the discussion of freedom itself.

When a student of any one of the arts has gained complete mastery over his medium, it is his own personality, expressed through his work, that will determine whether he is a true artist or not. If he has nothing of his own to add to the art he pursues, he will remain in pursuit of the true object of art; he may be a superb technician, but he will forgo the freedom of the artist. In other words, he will lack style.

The word *style* is seldom used in connection with dancing, in the sense just described. "Style" usually relates to a method of dressing the hair, or to the cut of a costume; whereas the word "personality" is freely employed. As the possessor of a "good personality" is uusally considered to have been born thus endowed, the general inference is that a person cannot develop a stage personality unless especially gifted by nature. This attitude does not allow for those born with dormant talents; and, if we substitute the word *style* for *personality*, it at once becomes evident that a good presence, although it may indeed be the result of natural gifts, can only be recognized on the stage by the way in which the performer presents himself to his audience, which is through the medium of his *personal style*. This presentation is an art in itself, and can be cultivated to the highest degree.

In painting and music we can recognize a certain style because of certain repetitions in the way that the artist or composer has handled his material. In dancing we are often dazzled by the physical and personal perfections of the performer, and nothing lasts long enough for us to consider its construction: we cannot hum a bar out of a *pas d'allégro* in order to reflect upon the dancer's personal style. When the performance is over, we are aware of the feeling of intense stimulation, and of a warmth as if we had just met an artist who is actually at work; so we attribute the whole experience to personality, as this social expression seems far more descriptive than the unemotional word *style.*

The student of ballet, however, should give great attention to the cultivation of style, which is utterly ignored by the vast majority of dancers and teachers.

An excellent illustration of the meaning of the word is afforded by Marie Taglioni (see p. 53) and the effect of her dancing on ballet, during her own career and at the present day. The study of contemporary literature and lithographs leaves us in little doubt that she had perfected the most bewitching and highly effective personal style. Nowadays there is a distinct tendency among dancers to try to copy the style of Marie Taglioni, when they are dancing, for example, in the second act of *Giselle;* but the attempt progresses no further than the imitation of separate poses, which are apt to occur both prefaced and followed by obviously present-day movements. The fact that Taglioni's entire system of movement must have been stylized in the same manner as the attitudes in which she posed for her portraits does not seem to have occurred to our contemporary dancers; in this respect alone, not only is it clear that they are doubtful as to the true meaning of the word *style*, but it also shows that they do not attribute to Taglioni what they do not possess themselves in the way of consistency of style. That they probably possess a greater technique than the dancers of the nineteenth century is beside the point; it should be remembered that in art there are no short cuts.

To attempt to recall the style of Taglioni cannot be undertaken lightly, nor practiced without the best of good taste. Perhaps it is more a question of the study of character than of style, but this will be investigated later on.

The perpetual view of the underneath of dancers' chins is largely due to a mistaken sense of style; to stick one's nose in the air is to confuse the dreary superiority of the department-store manager with the brilliant authority of the ballerina. When every member of the *corps de ballet* advances down the stage in this mistaken "grand manner," as far as the citizens in the stalls are concerned, not one of the girls has a face—only a chin. (For another cause of "chin-trouble," see pp. 18 and 31.)

A good style must not be confused with the development of mannerisms. Good style is possessed by the dancer who improves her dancing in a way that is hers alone: mannerisms result from the mechanical application of the same sets of formulas to all dance-movements.

A last word concerning the personal style of a dancer. Ballet students have been heard to criticize the choreography of *Giselle*, particularly

THREE ADAPTATIONS OF NATIONAL DRESS FOR BALLET

M. & Mme. Paul Taglioni: Paris, 1833.
Adaptation of Styrian Peasant Dress.
(from a contemporary painting)

Nursemaid & Coachman in "Pétrouchka."
Adaptation of Russian Peasant Dress.
from the design by Alexandre Benois. 1911.

The Dandy & a Peasant Girl in "Le Tricorne."
Adaptation of Spanish Costume by Pablo Picasso, 1919.
(from the original design)

the *adage* in the second act. "It may be very difficult," was the comment, "but it is also rather *dull.* How can you make anything out of such classroom steps?"—The answer to that question, of course, is the answer to another: viz., what is personal style? The *adage* in question begins with a very slow *développé à la seconde,* and is quite easy to recognize; if the reader will memorize this step, and then go and watch a great ballerina performing it as Giselle, the meaning of style should become perfectly clear. (An example of lack of style may be found on pp. 48–9.)

ii. On character

"The Joy of a *Monarch* for the news of a Victory, must not be express'd like the Extasie of a *Harlequin* on the Receipt of a letter from his Mistress. . . ." (Dryden, 1760.)

While collecting material for this book, I have been hunting for schools of dancing that include character classes, and I have drawn what is virtually a complete blank, except in those cases where classes are given teaching classical mime, which is of little general use, unless one is going to play, at least, the Prince's Friend in *Swan Lake,* or the part of some soloist in *The Sleeping Princess;* and here we recognize the seeds of further chin-trouble being sown. In our contemporary portrayals of royalty, the kings and queens, dukes, duchesses, and courtiers, instead of displaying that effortless dignity and grace compatible with their rank, usually give the impression of an overbearing superiority, with their noses well in the air. This is to confuse snobbishness with greatness, and will destroy the convincingness of any court scene.

In its finer form and under ideal conditions, the academic ballet training can be said to cover any field likely to be demanded of the dancer; but at the present time performances have shown that a company cannot function satisfactorily without dancers who have had or are given some instruction concerning the interpretation of character roles. However well Giselle and Albrecht dance together, the performance as a whole can be sadly impaired by surrounding groups of expressionless and unschooled courtiers in the first act, and flocks of bored, earth-bound Wilis in the second. Photographs taken during actual performances of *Giselle* are a revelation: during the mad scene a study of the groups of courtiers will usually reveal anything from boredom to the animation of a private conversation.

In contrast with this deplorable state of affairs, one photograph shows the puppet Petrouchka dying and bleeding sawdust on the fairground, surrounded by a crowd of revelers engrossed in watching the tragedy; the expression of each one is perfectly true to life and, ranging from the horror of the people in the front row to the curiosity of those craning their necks at the back, the group, were they dressed in everyday clothes, might represent the gathering at a street accident.

Consequently Petrouchka, with his sympathizers, will be able to give a greater performance than poor Giselle, with her uninterested courtiers and villagers; and we, the audience, will only realize why this was so when we chance to study action photographs, because we had eyes only for the principal performers during the course of the ballet.

Even if all dancers were suitably trained to acquit themselves well in the two ballets described above, there is still the question of the choreographer who wants to produce a ballet on (for the sake of an example) a Hungarian theme. He has first to set about training his dancers; they will be unable to grasp any of his movements unless he gives them special coaching first. This takes time and patience, and it is not really the choreographer's job. Even if the dancers had not learned the rudiments of Hungarian dancing, yet if they had been trained to pick up the main characteristics of national dancing in general, they would be far more adaptable. As it is, we see dancers performing czardas and jotas without any enjoyment; and substituting a kind of half-hearted polka for a spirited mazurka, and so on.

It is probably the limitations mentioned above that have caused so many of our contemporary choreographers to fall back on the mainly dramatic ballet, where an elaborate libretto is enacted by the dancers, during the course of which dances take place as a sort of relief from the dramatic action.

iii. Style in costume

The same factors that govern style in dancing also apply to *décor* and costumes. The quality for which we all search subconsciously is *subtlety*. There was a time when a tendency towards a too meticulous realism robbed the ballet of much of its magic; this was followed by the inevitable reaction, a harsh and heavy-handed form of sybolism that divorced the art of ballet from nature, whence it springs. Today both extremes are apparent; a performance of *Scheherazade* in the United States was remarkable for the introduction of real elephants on the stage; and most lovers of ballet are familiar with those uncomfortable "modernistic" designs which are the despair of the costumier and dancer alike.

In case the allusion to nature seems a little obscure, this section is illustrated with a drawing after Léon Bakst's original design for Vaslav Nijinsky in *Le Spectre de la Rose;* beside it is a drawing of the generally adopted modern version of this masterpiece. It is clear that Bakst studied nature, and he has so arranged his costume that the mysterious element of the rose is stressed, rather than its feminine associations. The colors used on Nijinsky's actual costume range from rose pink to shades of purple, red, and tawny brown. In contrast, one shade of sugar pink is used in the modern version; the main garment has become a kind of bathing-suit, and the headdress a boudoir cap. Whereas there is every excuse for altering the design of a costume that does not suit the wearer, this perfunctory approximation of a beautiful design is lamentable.

In keeping with this superficiality, the choreography has suffered much the same sort of change. Apart from Nijinsky's famous leap, which could be repeated by no one, with the exception of Stanislas Idzikowski, the emotional romanticism that inspired the entire conception has undergone the same modification as the costume. Losing oneself in the fascinating study of ballet tradition, one is apt to overlook the laws of nature on which that tradition is based.

STYLE IN COSTUME:
two versions of "Le Spectre de la Rose"

Vaslav Nijinsky as the Spirit of the Rose: after the design by Léon Bakst, 1911

A typical modern version of the same costume

CHAPTER X. PRACTICAL NOTES

i. On costumes and décor

Many of our contemporary ballet performances can be seen to fuller advantage during rehearsal than *en spectacle* on the stage. In an earlier chapter we have examined those individual occasions where a dancer appears brilliant in class but monotonous on the stage; we must take a broader view of the situation, however, when the subject concerns entire ballets and not merely the projection-powers of separate dancers.

It is quite obvious that bad performance may ruin a ballet; but bad decoration—that is, unsuitable costumes and *décor*—not only ruins the dancer's performance, but can also obscure the very structure of the choreography itself.

The two worst pitfalls for the ballet-designer are: (a) the failure to design costumes that are suitable for *movement*, and (b) the faulty use of color and design. Concerning note (a), many costume-designers fail to appreciate that the choice of material, and its cut, must be governed by a knowledge of human movement. For example, panniers, covered by heavy material, which look most impressive when worn by the static figure, look clumsy and absurd during a *pas d'allégro* (see sketches 1 and 2 opposite); moreover they reduce the wearer to a state of utter exhaustion. With more ethereal costumes, the deft addition of draperies with the swish of a paint-brush, which look so effective on the design itself, may prove a nightmare for the dancer, catching at his feet, and attaching themselves to projections of scenery. In both cases, the designer, the dancer, *and the dressmaker* should combine to see that the costume is effective, comfortable, practicable, and physically becoming to the wearer.

Regarding note (b), the elementary factors governing the use of color and design, shown in their simplest form in sketches 5, 6, and 7, are often entirely overlooked. Variations of the effect suggested by no. 7 may be used for a special purpose; but as an unconscious tendency, it may obscure much excellent choreography and confuse the dramatic action, while the value of the separate dancers themselves will be lost completely on the audience.

The confusion of outline in no. 7 can be caused in a number of ways, not only by the overloading of ornamentation on *décor* and costumes, or by the failure to consider the costumes in relation to the background; untheatrical or faulty stage-lighting, alone, can upset altogether an otherwise well-balanced scenic effect.

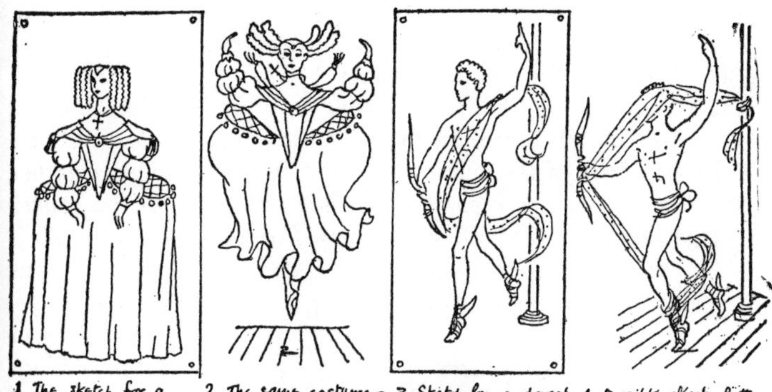

1 The sketch for a costume. 2. The same costume – in action. 3. Sketch for a draped figure. 4. Possible effect of the draperies in action.

Diagrams 5 - 6 - 7 prove a forgotten rule: dark colours show against a light background & vice versa: too much ornamentation, or too many similar colours, confuse the onlooker and obscure the dancer's movements.

8 The use of strong lighting will show up the dancer. Weak lighting will usually give the same effect as 7. above

9. "INTERPLAY" (sketched from the pit.)

Those who are unfamiliar with ballet practice-costumes should make an effort to see Jerome Robbins's American choreographic romp, *Interplay*. The *décor* (by Oliver Smith) consists of large expanses of cheerful, glowing colors, against which the movements of the simply clad dancers show clearly. (I was able to sketch the performers quite easily from the very back of the auditorium.) A more sophisticated version of the same precept may be seen in Frederick Ashton's beautiful *Symphonic Variations*, with *décor* by Sophie Fedorovitch.

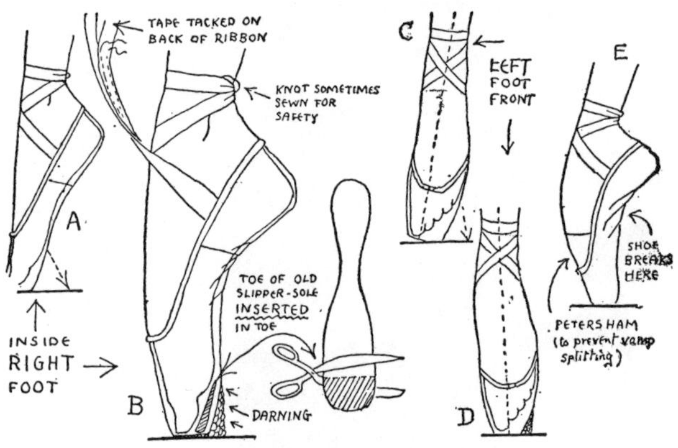

ii. On the comfort of ballet slippers

In the first chapter, the problems of the bow-legged dancer's feet have been mentioned, and a remedy promised. Fig. A, above, shows the tendency of this type of foot, which is a constant source of worry and muscular strain to the owner, not only because of its appearance but because it is so difficult to remain "on point." Fig. B shows a special addition to the routine darning, which combines with the use of a pad made from the sole of an old slipper to make the shoe far more comfortable, and improves the appearance of the foot into the bargain. Fig. C shows that the arrangement of toes on this type of foot is inclined to make the owner turn her ankle in an ugly and dangerous manner; D shows the remedy, by the addition of more darning. Fig. E shows the high instep of the close-legged dancer, whose shoe is inclined to break, as indicated; the only remedy here is to take an inner sole from an old shoe and stick it firmly inside the broken one. Where the vamp of the shoe is inclined to tear, this may be avoided in advance by the insertion of a piece of petersham ribbon, as shown. This will also relieve some of the tension on the sole. Lining the satin ribbons with tape has saved many a dancer from public ignominy, and applies to all types of foot (fig. B). Even if ballet shoes become easier to obtain, their price is the despair of the ballet student, so here is a way to prolong their life: when the blocks have become too soft, a useful expedient is to soak the interior with *straw-hat dye*, leaving it overnight to dry and harden.

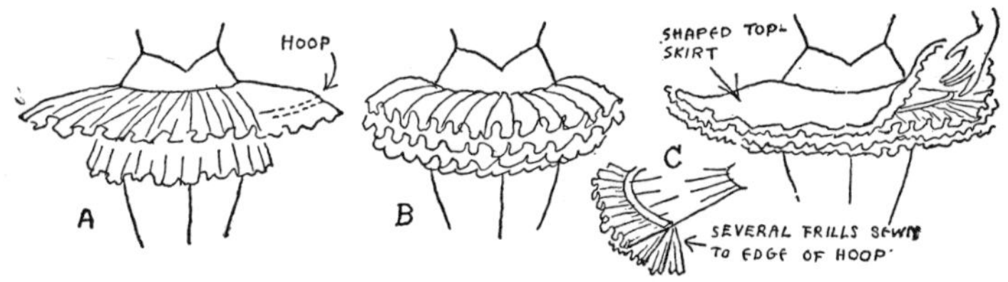

iii. On the construction and appearance of tutus

Although the *tutu* is such an indispensable item of ballet production, it is notable how seldom one sees this costume satisfactorily carried out. Sometimes the fault is in its design, sometimes in its execution. Fig. A, above, shows a *tutu* in which the wire hoop is too far from the wearer's hips; the stiffness having left the tarlatan underskirts, the result is depressing and untidy. B shows what is generally known as the powder-puff type of *tutu*—too short and too bulky. C shows a far more satisfactory and becoming arrangement; the hoop is not more

than 7 inches from the wearer's hips, and is edged with four frills, which give a pleasantly *bouffant* effect without the heavy dumpiness of B, and avoid the limpness of A. *Below*, fig. D shows the accepted silhouette for the contemporary classical dancer; F, a classical costume as worn at the Paris Opéra in 1860. E represents the misuse of both the former characteristics. The dancer's legs are neither hidden nor revealed, her figure is bowdlerized, and even the attempt at splendor has gone sadly astray. The general proportions, and the mixture of hair-style, head-dress, cloak, and fan, are an awful warning to the would-be designer.

iv. On making up

Fig. A shows a girl facing her mirror. She is going to make up for *Les Sylphides*. It will be seen that although her face is not remarkable for strength of feature, yet it is extremely pretty; she has medium coloring. B shows the same girl as she will appear on the stage having used a make-up which looked very nice in her dressing-room, but which disappeared under the strong stage lights. Eyebrows, chin, and eyes have vanished, leaving a mask of the type which some people hang on their walls, but which cannot register any expression whatever. The forehead appears narrow and receding, and this is caused partly by the dowdy hair-style (in fig. A the forehead looks quite adequate), and partly by the hideous angle of the wreath. There seems to be no division between neck and chin. C shows the same girl with a make-up that will make her look naturally beautiful on the stage, and will resemble her own appearance far more closely than B. The only real adjustment she has made to her face is to apply a flesh-tint over a little of the hair on the temples, to broaden the forehead. This is usually a far safer method than to attempt to make the face look narrower by applying shadow to the cheeks. The hair-style used in fig. C also helps to broaden the forehead by masking any undue roundness or heaviness about the lower part of the face.

Fig. D shows a type of make-up affected by those who hanker after slanting eyes, and it goes with a forbidding expression; this is splendid for a scene in an inferno, but is hardly suitable for a sylph. E shows the effect of a modish hair-style when affected by a sylph; she has to turn her back before one can see her wreath. The supercilious expression is suitable for an advertisement for cosmetics, but has no relation to ballet. (The original coiffure for the original sylphide can be seen in the sketch of Taglioni on p. 53; the later romantic coiffure of Spessivtzewa, on p. 46.) F: an improvement on the wig of the *danseur* in *Les Sylphides*, and for all romantic roles of this order; the wearer attaches a small roll of hair, exactly the color of his own, round the nape of his neck, as shown. This dispenses with the discomfort of a wig and the usually unbecoming hairline other than one's own.

A final generalization concerning make-up: in some companies the men are advised to wear dark lipstick, and the girls a paler shade. This is forgetting the effect of theatrical lighting, under the glare of which the girls would seem to have no mouths at all, and the men would possess the legendary ruby lips. The advice should be reversed.

v. On the arrangement of hair

The designer of costumes usually indicates the way in which he wants the hair to be arranged, on his design. Occasionally a wig solves the dancer's problem; but more often she is called upon to effect a complicated coiffure with her own hair. This may involve an interpretation of a modern design or of a drawing made many years ago. Here, then, are some general notes for the use of those who design coiffures and those who have to put them into practice.

The same considerations apply to the arrangement of hair as to the design of an entire costume. It is inadvisable to be pedantic when reproducing hair-styles of a bygone fashion, especially if it is a fashion that is comparatively recent, in which case an exact reproduction will impart an atmosphere of fustiness and general *démodé*. On the other hand, in the case of a period coiffure, an obvious intrusion of the present fashion will appear vulgar and out of place (see fig. E.): therefore a careful adaptation should be made by the designer and the dancer which escapes these two infringements of taste, but which brings out the best features of the wearer's face.

CURTAIN

INDEX AND DRAMATIC PERSONÆ

Academic technique, 6, 62–3
Acrobat, 5, 7
Adage (*adagio*), 21, 31, 37
Æsthetics: dancer's definition, 4; in training, 5
Allégro, temps d', 22
Ankles, 21, 30
Arabesque, 44, 45, 48, 49; distortion of, 45; Moorish, 44, 45; *penché*, 49
Argentina, La, 57
Arms: double-jointed, 28; exercise for, 29; in leaping, 28; long and short, 28–9; use of the, 24ff.
Arqué (formation of the legs), 20, 22, 64
Artist-dancer, the 7–8
ASHTON, FREDERICK, 76
Attaque, 12, 64
Attitude, devant, 34–5
Attitude (from *Les Sylphides*), 41
Auditorium, imaginary, 36–7
Aurora's Wedding, 62
Awkward dancers, 17
Awkward moments, 60

BAKST, LÉON, 73
Balance: in action, 32, 34; in partnering, 60; maintaining, 31
Ballerina, classification of the, 63–4
Ballet: company, 61; dramatic, 72; rehearsal, 74
Ballet-designer, pitfalls for the, 74
Ballets, classification of, 62–3
Ballon, 22
BARONOVA, IRINA, 15
Barre, la, 18, 19
BEAUMONT, CYRIL, W., 9–10, 13
BELLORI, GIOVANNI PIETRO, 65
BENOIS, ALEXANDRE, 70
BLASIS, CARLO, 24, 50–1
Bow-legged dancer, the 20, 22–3

CAHUSAC, 11
CAMARGO, MARIE, 50, 51
Carnaval, 63
CECCHETTI, ENRICO, 12, 13
Character (of the dancer), 14
Character-dancing, notes on, 68
"Chin-trouble," 69
Choreographer, problems of the, 51–3, 72
Choreography, 56–7, 73,74
Classical ballet, 62
Classical *tutu*, 67
Classifications, 62–6
Close-legged dancer, the, 20–1
Code of Terpsichore, The, 50–1
"Cold" dancer, the, 5,7, 52
Control, physical, 7, 12
COOMARASWAMY, ANANDA, 2
Coppélia, 63
Corps de ballet and ensemble work, 61
Costume: national, 70; notes on, 74–6; style in, 72–3
Critics, 3, 24
Croisée, 39
Croisée devant, derrière, 36, 37, 39
Czardas, 72

"Dancer's back," 18
Danseur, classification of the, 64
Darning of ballet-shoes, 76
Décor, notes on, 74–5
Deportment, 18
Développé à la quatrième devant, 34–5
DIAGHILEV, SERGE, 13
Directions of the body, the eight, 36–7
Double tours en l'air, 32
DRYDEN, 71
DUPRÉ, 51

Écartée, 36
Échappé, 21
Effacée, 36
Elevation, steps of, 34
Emotional content of music, 52
Entrechat, 6, 21, 22, 50
Épaulée, 37
Equilibrium, 31
"Expressionistic" dance, 6

FEDOROVITCH, SOPHIE, 76
Feeling (in dancing), 4–5, 6–7, 46–7
Feet, notes on, 76–7
Fifth position of the arms *en haut*, 27
FOKINE, MICHEL, 17, 53
Fouettés (in perspective), 33
FRANCA, CELIA, 40–1, 54–5

GARDEL, 24, 51
GARRICK, DAVID, 9

Giselle, 46, 51, 61, 63, 64, 67, 69, 71, 72
GLUCK, 9
GRAHN, LUCILLE, 26
Grand jeté en tournant, 39, 40–1
Grands battements, 22
"Greek" dancing, 6
GRISI, CARLOTTA, 13, 26
GORE, WALTER, 57

Hair, on the arrangement of, 79–80
Harmony of movement (in *pas-de-deux*), 61
Head, use of (in turning), 33

IDZIKOWSKY, STANISLAS, 13, 73
Individuality, 11, 12–13
Insensitivity, 6, 7–8
Insteps: high and low, 20, 22; tendons of the, 50
Interplay, 75
Interpretation, 40–1
Interpretative dancing, 46, 52, 56

Jarreté (formation of the legs), 20, 64
Jota, 72

KARSAVINA, TAMARA, 13, 61, 63

LANY, 50
Letters on Dancing (Noverre), 3, 9–10, 11, *and see* Noverre
Lifts, 58–60
"Line": in *arabesques*, 44–5; in dancing, 46–7

Maîtres-de-ballet, notes on, 10
Making up, notes on, 77–8
Malformation (of the legs), 20
MARINO, 50
MASSINE, LEONIDE, 12, 57, 66
Mazurka, 39–41, 54–5, 72
Mechanics (of dancing), 30
Mirror, arms and the, 25, 28
Misinterpretation, 6, 48–9
Modernistic designs, 72
"Muscle-bound," 18
Muscles, overdeveloped, 19
Musicality: demonstration of, 54–5; notes on, 50–3

Negro (rhythmical), 57
NIJINSKY, VASLAV, 22–3, 61, 63, 65, 66, 73
NOVERRE, JEAN GEORGES, 3, 9–10, 11, 20, 24, 46, 50, 57

Palais de danse, 57
Partnering, notes on, 58–61
Pas-de-deux, 6; from *Les Sylphides*, 58–9
Pas-de-quatre, notes on, 61
Passions, in dancing, 6, 7
PAVLOVA, ANNA, 14, 47, 66
PERROT, JULES, 13
Perspective: physical, 36–7; stage, 36–9
Petrouchka, 62, 70, 72
PICASSO, PABLO, 70
Pirouettes, 6
Pliés (in elevation), 34
Pointes, sur les, 20, 21, 22, 76
Point-shoes, notes on, 76–7
Polka, half-hearted, 72
Posés, 34–5
Practical notes, 74ff.
PREOBRAJENSKAYA, OLGA, 14–15
Pupils, 11–13

Quatrième: derrière, à la, 37; *devant, à la*, 36

Renversé, toure en: en dedans, 43; *en dehors*, 42
Rhythmical dancer, the, 56–7
RIABOUCHINSKA, TATIANA, 15
ROBBINS, JEROME, 57, 76
Romantic ballet, 62–3
Romantic *tutu*, the, 53, 67
Ronds de jambe, 21; and "*de bras*," 29

Scheherazade, 72
SCHOLES, PERCY A., 56
"Scientific" dancer, the, 12
Seconde, à la, 37
Second position of the arms, 26–8
SHAKESPEARE, WILLIAM, 9
Sissone en arrière, 34
Sleeping Princess, The, 63, 71
SMITH, OLIVER, 76
Soliste, the, 36, 38, 64
Spectre de la Rose, Le, 73
SPESSIVTZEWA, OLGA, 46
Splits, the, 45
Stagecraft, training in, 38
Stage: etiquette, 37; personality, 68; sense. 60; the Cecchetti, 38

STEVENSON, HUGH, 67
Style in dancing, notes on, 68–9, 71
Swan Lake, 48–9, 63, 67, 71
Swan Princess, the, 48–9, 63–4
Sylphide, La, 53
Sylphides, Les, 17, 39–41, 53–5, 58–9, 62, 63, 78–9
Symphonic Variations, 76

TAGLIONI, M. and MME PAUL, 70
TAGLIONI, MARIE, 24, 53, 69
Teaching, 11ff.
Team-work, 61
Temperament, 7–8
Terpsichore, 50
Time, tempi (in music), 20, 56–7
Tone: in *décor* and costumes, 74–6; in music, 52
TOUMANOVA, TAMARA, 15
Tradition, 66, 73
Training: basic, 18–23; musical, 50–3; subtlety in, 6
Tutus: notes on the construction of, 77–8; romantic and classical, 67
Types of dancer, 66

ULANOVA, GALINA, 67

Virtuoso, the technical, 12
VOLTAIRE, 9

Wilis, costume for a, 67

A NOTE ON THE TYPE

This book was set on the Monotype in *Bodoni*, a printing-type so called after Giambattista Bodoni, a celebrated printer and type designer of Rome and Parma (1740–1813). Present-day *Bodoni* type faces were adapted from the original Bodoni designs and were cut for Monotype machine typesetting in 1911. Bodoni's innovations in printing-type style were a greater degree of contrast in the "thick and thin" elements of the letters, and a sharper and more angular finish of details.